"With loss and grieving a part of every
when a child grieves and how to help them recover. When ...,
children scrape their knee I know how to clean and patch. But
when their heart is bruised it's a different situation. Caring is first
aid for the heart—theirs and yours. A must read for every parent."

> —Tom Hoerner, Executive Liaison, National Fathers'
> Resource Center, Fathers for Equal Rights, Inc., and
> author, *The Ultimate Survival Guide for the Single Father*

"Now I can hand both parents and professionals a book that, in a
readable and sensitive way, presents childhood grief through
developmental eyes. Wakenshaw picks up where the play therapy
session ends with meaningful, hands-on activities that help children
heal their grief."

> —Kathy Dallman, MFCC, Registered Play Therapist,
> Bothell, WA

"A very moving, straightforward tool, to help both parents and
children heal through the grief process."

> —Martha Faulkner, child and family therapist specializing
> in adoption issues, Seattle, WA

"As the parent of a child with autism, I believe the most effective
form of therapy extends from the clinician's office into the home
where the young child spends most of his time. This book should
be on every parent's reading list to help their child through the
grieving process, whether it's the loss of a family pet, coping with
feelings when a best friend moves away, or the death of a family
member. *Caring for Your Grieving Child* is like having a child
therapist with you at home, sharing with you the tools she uses in
healing your own child."

> —Raheena Charania, freelance magazine writer (Seattle's
> Child, Eastside Parent) Editor/Contributing Writer (FEAT
> of Washington Autism Resource Guide)

"Incredibly practical and enlightening. As a mother of two, I only wish I had had this book sooner. Not only does it provide excellent advice for how to assist your child through the grieving process, but it also insightfully facilitates healthy parent-child communications throughout life."

> —Terry Frishman, Columbia MBA, mother of Ivy & Becca Gluck

Comments on the author's previous book, *This Child of Mine: A Therapist's Journey*

"No one will remain unmoved by psychotherapist Martha Wakenshaw's *This Child of Mine: A Therapist's Journey,* an account of extremely disadvantaged children who have been failed by their parents, the child welfare system, or both."

> —*Publisher's Weekly*

"A beautiful book: sensitive and luminous."

> —Jonathan Kozol, author, *Savage Inequalities, Amazing Grace,* and *Ordinary Resurrections*

"Martha Wakenshaw's *This Child of Mine: A Therapist's Journey* feels like love filling the immense hole of our broken hearts from what has happened to so many of our children. Read this book and rejoice for Wakenshaw's retrieving these thrown-away stories. This is the true alchemy of love."

> —Sharon Doubiago, author, *Hard Country, South American Mi Hija,* and *The Book of Seeing with One's Own Eyes.*

Caring *for* Your Grieving Child

ENGAGING ACTIVITIES FOR DEALING WITH LOSS AND TRANSITION

Martha Wakenshaw, MA, LMHC

FOREWORD BY HERMAN M. FRANKEL, MD

NEW HARBINGER PUBLICATIONS, INC.

Distributed in the U.S.A. by Publishers Group West; in Canada by Raincoat Books; in Great Britain by Hi Marketing, Ltd.; in South Africa by Real Books, Ltd.; in Australia by Boobook; and in New Zealand by Tandem Press.

Copyright © 2002 by Martha Wakenshaw
New Harbinger Publications, Inc.
5674 Shattuck Avenue
Oakland, CA 94609

Cover design © 2002 by Poulson/Gluck
Edited by Karen O'Donnell Stein
Text design by Tracy Marie Carlson

ISBN 1-57224-306-6 Paperback

New Harbinger Publications' Web site address: www.newharbinger.com

04   03   02

10   9   8   7   6   5   4   3   2   1

First printing

For the children

Contents

Part 2
Healing Play Exercises

Foreword

Readers of this much-needed and practical book, *Caring for Your Grieving Child: A Guide for Parents,* will have occasion to give thanks, again and yet again, to author Martha Wakenshaw.

First of all, thanks for making it clear that losses big and little occur often in the lives of children, and that children, as well as grownups, can understand that dealing with loss is a basic life skill that all of us can cultivate. Pets die, are hit by cars, run away, or are euthanized; friends move away; such possessions as jewelry, purses, and wallets somehow disappear; children lose familiar positions, memberships, and connections; they lose beloved pals, teammates, and teachers. Learning that grieving is important, natural, and permissible, even when a loss appears to be minor, can help children (and adults) develop the resources for dealing effectively with the catastrophes, setbacks, and disappointments that are part of life.

Second, thanks for presenting the accessible information and practical tools that distressed grownups need when family members experience life-changing losses. So often, when we adults are overwhelmed by the emotions that we feel in response to such family events as death, or divorce, or development of incapacitating chronic illness, we become aware that we don't know what to do to help ourselves cope. At the same time, we are likely to become less sensitive than we would otherwise be to the needs of our children. Further, so often when we do begin to recognize that our children are suffering, we become aware that we really do not know what we can do to help them grieve their losses.

Third, thanks for showing all of us that people need people, at times of sadness as well as times of joy. Our grieving children benefit from having us attend to them lovingly and wisely, sometimes to interact with them and sometimes to protect their solitude. In the same way, we need social support from grownups we love and trust if we are to be able to give ourselves permission to do our own grief work. If our children (and we) are to respond to loss in ways that help us grow in wisdom and learn to love better, we have to do the work for ourselves; but we really do not, and perhaps we really cannot, do it by ourselves.

As a pediatrician, I've had the good fortune to spend the past thirty-five years learning from children and grownups who have found themselves confronting challenges, crossroads, and losses in their lives. My special interest, of course, is in children: protecting them from harm, helping them and their families deal with disruptions of their lives and their well-being, and facilitating their healthy growth and development.

During the past decade, my colleagues and I have directed our attention primarily to working with people as they cope with the most commonly occurring traumatic event in the lives of American children: parental separation and divorce. From work done by others, and from our own work with children and their parents who have allowed us into their homes and their lives, we have been learning what hurts and what helps.

Parental divorce, like the death of a loved one, is devastating, even when the divorcing or the dying provides relief from unremitting pain and suffering. Often, the parent caring for the child feels so helpless at not knowing what to do that the question, "What shall I do?" is not even asked. In *Caring for Your Grieving Child: A Guide for Parents,* Martha Wakenshaw, as a loving parent, a caring clinician, and a thoughtful guide, raises and addresses the important questions: How can I get some insight into what my child is experiencing? How can I support my child's grieving process? How can I recognize when my child needs professional help? What will help me maintain my emotional balance?

It helps to remember that children who are old enough to love are old enough to grieve. It helps to remember that grieving a loss is a normal and healthy process. It helps to remember that when their grief work is supported and facilitated, children (and other people) who have experienced painful losses—*grievous* losses—can heal, and can continue their life journeys better able than before to deal with setbacks and losses. It helps to remember that parents can support their children's impulse and capacity to do the work of grieving a loss, work that occurs again and yet again, work that can be regarded as taking place repeatedly in terms of thoughts (cognitive domain), feelings (affective domain), actions (behavioral domain), and meaning (spiritual domain). It helps to know that we are not alone.

And it helps to have an experienced, knowledgeable, loving guide, and a guidebook like the one you are holding in your hands.

—Herman Frankel, MD
Director, The Divorcework Center at Portland
Health Institute, Inc.

Introduction

As our three-year-old daughter raced cars under our feet, my husband and I discussed the decline of our beloved family dog, Pippin. "She seems to be in a lot of pain," I said. "I wonder if it's time to put her down."

Intent on washing the dishes, we didn't notice that Molly Rose had stopped zooming her cars about and was hanging on our every word. "Mommy, Pippin's old. Are we going to throw her away?"

My daughter's words sounded a triple alarm for me: Death is not a subject to discuss casually in front of a child. Code words like "put her down" are misleading. And my daughter was receiving an incorrect message—when something is old, you dispose of it. I realized that children are more vulnerable and in need of extra care during times of loss.

So what is loss? Loss is not always defined as a death or divorce. Loss is the experience of something meaningful being taken away, an experience that threatens a person's sense of comfort and well-being, and creates uncomfortable physical and psychological feelings.

Preschoolers are more likely to experience the death of a pet or a grandparent than any other loss, with the exception of divorce.

Other losses such as separating from home and going off to kinder-garten, or a parent starting to work, are also significant to a young child and are often overlooked as we focus on more "profound" losses.

For older children, the death of beloved pets or grandparents, and the experience of divorce, remain leading causes of loss; how-ever, other losses can include the death of siblings, parents, or friends. Exclusion from a popular peer group and starting middle school are also situations that carry feelings of loss and grief.

For all children loss is a natural but extremely difficult part of life. Children depend on consistency and stability in their environ-ment in order to reach developmental milestones. Loss and grief can temporarily derail normal child development.

Who Should Read This Book

Caring for Your Grieving Child is geared toward parents and care-givers of children ages three to nine, but many of the concepts will be helpful to children of all ages and to adults who are grieving unre-solved childhood losses.

The loss of a loved one can be especially difficult for young children. Busy with the developmental tasks of expanding their social skills and emotional attachments, they tend to find special delight in befriending an animal or developing a loving relationship with a grandparent. The tighter the bond, the harder the loss. For children, losing a beloved person or pet makes them aware of their own vul-nerability to death and the inevitable death of those they love and care about.

If you are uncertain of how much or what to say to a grieving child or even need some help determining whether your child is grieving, reading this book will give you practical tips for dealing with these challenging issues. It is likely that you are sharing your child's grief over his or her loss or that you are both grieving the same loss. This book is written in a way that takes into account how painful and difficult the grieving process is. In times of loss and grief, a simple and compassionate approach that promotes healing works best. I have tried to provide you with some information and tools that can help.

How to Use This Book

If your child is actively grieving you might find it most useful to locate your topic of interest and concern in the table of contents and read just that part of the book. When things have eased up, reading the book as a whole may be useful to help you understand how ages and stages and play figure into a child's expression of grief.

Part 1 provides a basic overview of childhood grief as it relates to child development. Part 2 gives specific and user-friendly play activities for you to do at home. These play activities are adapted from the tools that professional child and play therapists use to treat grieving children. The book can also be read as a preventive measure, so you will be well prepared to handle a loss, should one affect your child some time later.

You will find that this book is unique in that it combines solid information on child development and tried-and-true play, art, and journaling exercises to help your child through the grieving process. You'll find several checklists that can help you determine whether your child is grieving and how losses affect his or her grieving process. Since you probably identify with or share in your child's grief, I have included some short journaling exercises that can be used to help you sort out your own feelings.

The Power of Play

Children's play is a great healer. I have devoted two chapters to specific play exercises that are inexpensive and can be done at home. These play techniques are modified versions of some of the interventions I have found most helpful when working with children in my sixteen years as a child and family therapist.

Play is one of the best ways I know of for children to come to grips with a loss. A child's work is play. Truly, children learn best by hands-on experience. Playing serves many vital functions, including testing reality in the safety of the play world. In play children can be at the control switch of their own fears as they experiment with happy and unhappy endings. Play also develops creative thinking, paves the way for organized and complex thinking, and helps children work through complex and confusing feelings. Research shows that play therapy is one of the most effective interventions for grieving children. Play therapy is sometimes used in conjunction with other types of mental health treatment, such as cognitive behavioral therapy.

In this book you will learn how to facilitate specific types of play that can help provide resolution for your child around such losses as a divorce or the death of a pet, grandparent, parent, sibling, or friend. You will also find information outlining how certain types of play can work with certain feelings associated with these losses, such as sadness, anger, betrayal, and disappointment.

Ages and Stages

It is helpful to look at loss through the lens of child development. The development of the child is threefold: body, mind, and spirit. All ages and stages have an attendant physical, mental, and spiritual growth component.

A three-year-old thinks quite differently about death than a seven-year-old does. A preschooler has a less refined command of language, understanding of feelings, and ability to think logically than a nine-year-old does. As the brain develops so do logical thinking and comprehension of emotions. It is critical that you recognize where your child is in the stages of development and meet him or her at the appropriate level of functioning. As your child moves through different developmental stages and acquires more sophisticated methods of self-expression, including language, expressive arts, and play that symbolizes real-life events, you will see a shifting perspective on the subject of loss and death.

At age three my daughter, Molly Rose, believed that death was reversible—that when our dog died he would wake up again and return to our family. Molly Rose packed dry food and a bottle of water for Pippin to take with him to heaven. As is typical of most three-year-olds, my daughter ascribed lifelike qualities to the deceased. According to Molly Rose, Pippin would continue to eat, breathe, and play after he died.

Conversely, my seven-year-old stepson had a more realistic handle on the death of Pippin. He understood that when Pippin died he was gone for good. The finality of the situation was hard for Patrick to accept. Like many children his age, he saw death as cold, empty, and lonely, and he feared for his own mortality.

As Molly Rose's perspective shows, preschoolers are masters of magical thinking. Euphemistic statements about death, overheard in adult conversation, can turn young children's ideas about death into full-blown fears that may result in eating and sleeping disturbances, acting out, withdrawal, or the development of phobias. This book will help you learn to talk about loss in ways that your child can understand.

Why I Wrote This Book

Children today are faced with more loss than children of past generations. Divorce remains the leading cause of childhood depression. The American Academy of Child and Adolescent Psychiatry reports that as many as 5 percent of all children in our country, or 3.4 million children, experience one or more episodes of clinical depression during their childhood (Fassler and Dumas 1997).

I wrote this book for Jason, Riley, and Sarah, among the children you will read about in this book. I wrote this book for their parents, who despite their best efforts were ill-equipped to help their children grieve a divorce or the death of a loved one. I wrote this book because more children are becoming depressed at an earlier age and this can be prevented.

Grief and depression, as you will learn, are two different things. Grief is an active process that is a natural part of the human life cycle. Grieving is a method that humans use to heal. Depression is grief that has gotten stuck. The more tools you have to help your child grieve, the less likely he or she is to become depressed.

I am a children's mental-health professional, but first I am a mother and stepmother. I know what it's like to be torn apart when your children's pet dies, or to experience their tears when they are teased or bullied or go through other "everyday losses." Our hearts are entwined with those of our children. I wrote this book with the heart of a mother and the mind of a caring professional.

You

You know yourself and your child best. Rely on your personal, religious, and spiritual values and beliefs to help guide you when you are relating to your child in times of grief. Allow yourself to grieve and you will be doing a great service to your child. Letting your child see you grieve gives him or her permission to experience a natural life process with less fear.

The more directly that your child can get in touch with his or her feelings of grief, the less likely it will be for his or her to have complicated or unresolved grief, which can linger on into the adult years and arrest developmental stages. Children who are supported by a loving and caring parent who can hear all of their feelings are most likely to heal from the grief over a death or loss of a loved one.

Molly Rose's Resolution

You may be wondering how the story of Molly and her little dog ended. Our daughter gave Pippin a kiss good-bye with a parting gift of dry food and a water bottle to take on his journey to heaven. As Molly Rose's dad left for the vet with Pippin wrapped in a special blanket, we cried and talked about our fond memories of the dog and how death is a natural part of life—just as the trees lose their leaves every winter, spring always returns with the promise of new life. The next day, we placed a bouquet of flowers on Pippin's kennel before retiring it to the basement.

Children such as Molly Rose who experience a sense of closure around a loss tend to heal from their grief more quickly than those who do not. Years later, when Molly's cat, Kniksu, died, she was able to implement similar rituals to gain closure. With her father's assistance, she made a grave site for the cat at the edge of our garden. She collected and set out pictures of Kniksu and lit a candle in her memory. Three months later, Molly came to me and said, "Mom, I'm ready to get a new cat!"

Part 1

Understanding Childhood Grief and Helping Your Child Heal

1

Understanding Your Child's Grief: An Overview

Karen, age three, caught me off guard when she stomped into my office, flung open the doors to the dollhouse, and threw the mother and father dolls out of the house, saying, "No mommies or daddies can live here. Just kids!"

I had been told that this child was grieving her parents' divorce. I expected a bundle of tears, not a ball of rage. But children express their grief in many ways. It is not always sadness that you will see in your grieving child. Anger is an emotion that is often overlooked in the child's grief process.

Emotions in children who are grieving may run high or low or in between, depending on your child's temperament or emotional temperature. A naturally withdrawn child will tend to turn inward with his or her grief and crave privacy. An extroverted child may find relief in talking about the loss. But there are no hard-and-fast rules when it comes to grieving. Expect the unexpected. Uncharacteristic behavior in your child goes with the territory. So, while your child may attempt to maintain his or her usual way of coping with an upset, a significant loss that triggers a grief response can be overwhelming and bring about unexpected behavioral changes.

Below are some signs that your child may be grieving:

* A marked change in eating and sleeping patterns: your child sleeps and/or eats more or less than he or she used to.

* Regression to earlier stages of development: your child suddenly wants his or her baby blanket back, even though it has been in storage for years.

* A loss of interest in previously pleasurable activities: your budding ballerina no longer has any interest in attending dance classes.

* Extreme tiredness: your child is constantly complaining that he or she is tired.

* An increase in angry and aggressive behavior: your child has sudden and uncharacteristic bouts of anger.

* An increase or decrease in affectionate behavior: your child becomes overly clingy or withdrawn.

* A preoccupation with morbid thoughts: your child becomes overly interested in death.

The Anatomy of Attachment and Loss

A newborn's first developmental task is to bond with his or her mother and father. This parent-child dance has everything to do with the parent picking up the child's cues and responding to his needs right away. A baby fusses and is fed. A baby cries and is held.

As children grow older they can fulfill more and more of their own basic needs. They learn how to feed themselves and dress themselves. They become more independent and start to separate from the parent. However, with the gain that accompanies each developmental milestone comes loss associated with leaving behind each developmental stage. John Bowlby, one of the best-known and well-respected authorities on attachment and separation, believes that, for a child, grief is always about losing something or having something taken away (1969).

When a loss such as a divorce or the death of a pet occurs, the child finds himself on unsteady ground. While they are ever increasingly separating from their parents, a child still needs to know that his parents are there for him. The ongoing process of changing and developing both physically and emotionally makes childhood grieving different from adult grieving—and harder to bear.

Here are some statements made by children who had experienced a loss:

I have a hurt in my heart. —Emily, age 3

I can't feel anything. —Aaron, age 7

It's like eating cake with no frosting. —Molly, age 9

I'm freaked out 'cause I can't think anymore, everything's all mixed up. —Jason, age 7

Everything is like black all the time. —Jim, age 5

I'm so tired. It's like I can't wake up. —Jenna, age 6

I've noticed that when children talk about loss, they grope for words and have a hard time expressing themselves. Their statements are poignant and, at times, heartbreaking, but I am left with a sense that there is a lot more going on behind the words. Looking at our children's play can give us the most information about how they are really feeling.

The Importance of Play

Play is the child's natural and primary way of expressing herself. Although we can learn quite a bit about the child's feelings by observing changes in behavior patterns such as sleeping, eating, and activity level, we can learn in more specific detail what is going on in our child's emotional world through the language of play.

Emily's Story: Playing Out Her Grief

Four-year-old Emily was delighted with the antics of her six-month-old baby sister, Rose. Emily quickly learned how to make her baby sister giggle. Emily enjoyed helping her mother change the baby's diapers and feed her a bottle before naptime. When Rose died of SIDS, Emily stopped eating and began speaking in baby talk, something she had not done in over a year. The only thing she would say was, "I have a hurt in my heart." But Emily's play revealed to her parents much more precisely what she was feeling.

Emily began to take a new interest in her dolls. It was as if she was transferring her affections for Rose to her dolls. In fact, doll play was about the only thing Emily was interested in doing. Since Rose's arrival, Emily had neglected her dolls, but now she couldn't get enough of them. Emily spent hours clothing and feeding her favorite doll. She paid careful attention to keeping the doll warm by wrapping it in blankets, as she had seen her mother do so often with her baby sister. She slept with her doll and would whisper to it, "Everything is okay. Mommy is here."

Emily asked her mom and dad when Rose would be coming home. She became angry and threw a tantrum when her mother talked about putting Rose's crib and bottles away. Emily made use of her toy doctor's kit and gave her doll "magic shots" that would keep her alive forever. Emily slept with her doll at night, assuring her that "no monsters will get you."

What Is Emily Trying to Say through Her Play?

Emily clearly believed that her sister had just gone away for a while and would be back. She felt that if she nurtured her dolls enough, everything would be okay. By transferring her affections for her deceased sister to her dolls, Emily was managing her feelings of deep sadness and hurt. She was playing out her grief in the only way she knew how. And by playing the role of the ever-present mother with her doll babies, Emily was reassuring herself that her mother would not go away and die as Rose had.

Despite her parents' explanation that death was final, Emily is unable to understand this concept. At age four she believed that death is reversible. No amount of logic would persuade her otherwise. At this stage of development, she simply needed to work out her fantasies and feelings through her play.

Jason's Story: Playing through Divorce

Seven-year-old Jason's parents had recently divorced, and Jason was having trouble understanding how his parents could do such a thing to him. Since they had divorced, Jason and his brother and sister now had to split their time between two homes. When he said, "Everything is all mixed up," he meant this quite literally. Boxes were still stacked in his room at his mother's house, waiting to be unpacked, when he visited his father's house, he would often forget to bring his baseball mitt for practice.

Jason was in the first grade, and he prided himself on his ability to read at the third-grade level. But after the divorce, it was as if someone had "switched his brain off." Jason was still reading, but he no longer remembered what he had read. He was failing his reading comprehension tests. "I just can't think anymore," he complained.

Jason became uncharacteristically methodical in his play. His parents were used to seeing their son as a free spirit who liked to "mess around" with his Legos; he would spend his time building imaginative space stations and playing out scenes from outer space with his little Lego men. But, since the divorce, he no longer experimented in the freewheeling way he used to. Instead, Jason would carefully pick through his Lego pieces and construct little square houses. Although he would sometimes put a fence around the houses, these buildings were not typical houses—they had no windows, doors, or plants around them. Jason's dwellings looked more like prisons than homes.

What Is Jason Trying to Say through His Play?

Jason felt like his world had been turned upside down. His normal routines had been disrupted. He couldn't remember when he had baseball practice or whether his mom or his dad would be taking him. After a while he gave up trying to sort it out and would leave his mitt at one house or the other. As a result, his mitt was never where he needed it. The age of seven is when logical thinking really kicks in for kids, so Jason was upset to find that he could no longer concentrate or "think anymore."

The tenor of Jason's play changed dramatically as he attempted to signal his parents that his life was a chaotic mess and he was feeling very much out of control. By his painstaking construction of Lego houses that resembled prisons, Jason was communicating his desperate need for control. Playing in this controlled manner gave him a way to feel in charge of something.

Jason's parents picked up on their son's cues and learned how to engage him in play so that he could express his feelings. Eventually he again became the old Jason who delighted in himself and his accomplishments.

What Do I Say to My Grieving Child?

Parents are often unsure of what or how much to say about death to their child. Don, the father of five-year-old Alex, commented, "I couldn't anticipate my own feelings around my mother's terminal cancer, let alone what my son was going through. The sadder I became, the more my son acted out and demanded my attention. I felt angry even though I knew Alex was just being a kid. It took me a while to recognize that my son was grieving too. When we talked openly about the impending death, things got a lot better."

It is a natural inclination to protect one's child from harm, and many parents believe that a frank discussion of death will emotionally damage their child. They may worry about the child's emotional backbone and how much information he can handle. Should he go to the funeral? How much can he understand? The responses to these questions will depend on the child's age and stage of development.

Three- to five-year-olds often view death through rose-colored glasses, believing that the deceased continues to live. However, this does not make the young child immune to feelings of sadness, guilt, and anger about the loss.

Five- to seven-year-olds tend to have an understanding of cause and effect and begin to grasp the idea that death is caused by illness or accident. Still, they may view death as reversible and believe that they have the power to make the deceased return to life if they wish hard enough. Children in this age group often feel that they are to blame for a death or loss.

Seven- to nine-year-olds' concept of death is closer to that of adults in that they view death as permanent. However, children in this age group grapple, in a much more concrete way, with fear about their own mortality and possible abandonment. Kids in this group may ask difficult questions, such as "Is there a heaven? Is there a hell?" "What does God look like?" and "If there is a God, how could He or She do this?"

It is important to use clear, concise language consistent with your child's developmental perspective on death. Stick to the facts. Avoid both complex explanations of death and sugar-coated responses. Try not to use euphemisms, words that do not accurately represent death. Words such as "sleeping," "resting," and "gone away" are some examples of inaccurate explanations of death. These vague words will confuse your child and leave much to her imagination, creating more questions than answers.

For example, one well-meaning mother told her seven-year-old son that his beloved cat, Sparkles, was "going to sleep forever." The child began to dread bedtime, fearing that he, too, would go to sleep forever. A well-intentioned father told his five-year-old daughter, "Honey, we're losing Grandma." The child responded enthusiastically, "Let's go find her, Dad!"

In children ages three to nine, the grieving cycle often takes the form of protest, pain, and hope. Protest is similar to the adult's stage of denial. Kids will act out more forcefully with actions, play, and words in protesting a loss.

The pain stage in children corresponds to that of anger in adults. It is a stage of intense feelings, including sadness, anger, betrayal, guilt, and other emotions. The hope stage is similar to the stage of acceptance in adults. Once the protest and pain stages have been worked through, hope for new beginnings is the lasting result.

Don't expect to see a linear progression through these stages in your child's healing process. Grief is cyclical and different stages of grieving may appear at different times in your child's development. For example, when my daughter was grieving the death of our dog, she went from pain to protest to pain to protest to hope and back again. It can be difficult for parents to see their child moving through the stages of grief in what seems like a never-ending cycle. Remember, though, that your child is not defined by his or her feelings. Your child is resilient and will eventually come to a place of hope.

Put Yourself in Your Child's Shoes

Do you remember the first significant loss that you experienced as a child? How old were you? Where were you living? *How did you feel?*

It is natural to want to forget painful losses and block them out of our minds. It is also common for people to minimize losses, saying things like "It really wasn't that bad when my dad moved out of the house when I was seven. At least I still had my mom." In order to jog our memories of a painful experience, putting ourselves back in that time and place can help. Try to remember what grade you were in. What time of year was it? What smells do you associate with the loss—a certain perfume, perhaps, or the smell of autumn leaves.

It is important for us, as parents, to remember how we felt as children and how the adults around us helped us or didn't help us work through the pain of grief. In remembering, we bring our life experience and maturity to our interpretation of past painful events. A clearer, more mature perspective may shine light on an old, unresolved loss that has created a feeling of unrest in us. When we remember our childhood experiences of loss, we allow ourselves to be more compassionate and more understanding of our child's needs.

My first memory of loss is of being hospitalized for two weeks when I was three years old. At the age of three, I was still learning to be independent and not count on my parents for everything. I was used to playing with other children while keeping an eagle eye on my mother, secure in the knowledge that she was still there, like a safe harbor. At this age, the invisible umbilical cord between parent and child is very much intact and as important to the child's fundamental feeling of security as is an astronaut's lifeline to the spaceship.

The ride to the hospital was an experience that I will never forget. Like most young children, I experienced my world through my senses. The sunlight was bright and made intricate patterns through the leafy trees that hung overhead as my father drove me to the hospital. The smell of autumn leaves came wafting through the car window. I remember the feeling of comfort I got from my father's strong hand in mine. I had a hollow feeling in my stomach and a lump in my throat as I recalled the image of my mother sitting on the front steps with my three brothers waving good-bye, the echo of their voices fading as we pulled out of the driveway. I felt like I was leaving home forever.

Getting in touch with our childhood memories can help us put ourselves in our child's shoes, so we can better understand what he or she is experiencing.

Common Questions from Concerned Parents:

Q: How do I know that my child isn't seriously depressed?

A: If three or more of the signs and symptoms of grief (see page 10) are still present and disruptive of your child's normal functioning after a two-week period, your child may be depressed and you should arrange a professional consultation with your pediatrician or a child mental-health specialist.

Note: If your child is preoccupied with death and morbidity for more than one week or makes statements like "I wish I were dead," or "I wish I had never been born," it is essential that you seek professional help immediately, even if no other signs or symptoms persist.

Q: Will my child ever get over the death of her sister?

A: Most children are more resilient than we think and do learn how to manage their grief. The majority of children do get over a significant loss, with caring and consistent support from adults. However, children will tend to re-grieve the loss on anniversaries of the loss, on special occasions, and at certain developmental stages.

Q: My child has basically stopped eating and is having trouble sleeping. Should I force him to eat? Should I worry about his lack of sleep?

A: Eating and sleeping are natural functions that we can't force on a child. Unless your child is losing a significant amount of weight, such as three or more pounds in a month, he is probably okay; however, if you have any concern at all, check with your family doctor. Sleep disturbance can cause a child to feel cranky and overstressed. If your child has trouble sleeping for more than a few days and none of your tried-and-true methods for helping your child get to sleep are working, I would recommend consulting your pediatrician.

Q: I can't stand to see my little girl cry. What can I do?

A: It is extremely difficult for parents to watch their children grieve. Try to identify and express your own feelings in an appropriate way. Crying is a healthy way to grieve. It is okay for a parent to cry in front of his or her child. Showing children that we are human and have feelings gives them permission to express their feelings.

Q: My child doesn't seem to be showing any emotion. Is that abnormal?

A: Children grieve in their own ways on their own timelines. It is not abnormal for a child to respond to a loss by showing a lack of emotion. She may be in a state of shock and may be using emotional numbing as a defense mechanism to prevent scary and overwhelming feelings from surfacing. If the absence of feeling persists, your child will need help expressing the feelings that are percolating beneath her emotionless presentation.

Many more issues will be covered in subsequent chapters, such as the appropriateness of taking a child to a funeral or memorial service, the ways children of different ages think of death, and the ways parents can help.

Ten Ways to Help Your Child Through the Grief Process

1. First find out what *you* are feeling.

2. Use accurate language to explain the loss.

3. Assure your child that he or she will continue to be loved and cared for.

4. Reestablish normal household routines.

5. Allow your child to express a full range of emotions.

6. Give your child the message that all of his or her feelings are okay.

7. Encourage your child to say good-bye to the person, pet, or situation being lost.

8. Use play and expressive arts to help your child express his or her feelings.

9. Help your child connect with community, through church, school, scouts, or other groups.

10. Draw upon personal rituals, and spiritual and religious beliefs.

During times of acute grieving, I keep them posted on our refrigerator door as a helpful reminder. Try posting this list in a central place in your home. These ten ways to help your child will be explained in detail throughout this book.

Although parents cannot be expected to do the work of trained mental-health professionals, parents do know their kids best and can help their children cope with their grief before it turns into depression. Later in this book you will learn some of the techniques that play therapists use to help children through their grieving process, and you will learn what your child is telling you through his or her symbolic play. As a play partner and parent, you will have an important role in your child's healing.

Although times of grief may seem intolerable and insurmountable, hope and healing always come in time. Just as the human body is equipped with an immune system to fend off disease, our emotional body is also thus equipped. With the help of this immune system, we tend to move out of painful situations and into stages of comfort and peace. The human instinct is always to move toward health, both mental and physical.

2

Children Grieve, Too

The way in which we perceive the emotional life of children has radically changed over time, as new information on child development has become available. Researchers have made many groundbreaking discoveries regarding the importance of early learning and how it affects later physical, intellectual, and emotional development.

Past and Present Theories of Child Development

The predominant theories around child development in the past focused on the child's intellect, or the cognitive process. Numerous studies were conducted, detailing the child's cognitive development from birth to age eighteen. However, research into the emotional life of the child was widely neglected. In fact, as recently as 1980 many researchers believed that children were incapable of experiencing the wide range of emotions that adults feel. Some child specialists believed that children were too emotionally immature to grieve.

Not only do we now know that children are capable of experiencing emotions like grief, we see various degrees of intensity that match or supersede an adult's depth of feeling. Children are not as adept as adults at expressing their feelings in words, but if we look closely and pay careful attention to children's behavior and play, we can see that the feelings they experience are quite sophisticated and numerous.

What Kinds of Childhood Loss Are Most Common?

It is wonderful that we now know so much about a child's emotional functioning because children today are likely to experience different types of loss and at a much greater frequency than did children of earlier generations. Below are some of the kinds of losses commonly experienced by children.

Divorce

Divorce is often cited as a leading cause of childhood depression, so it's important to look at the increasing divorce rate in our society and its impact on children. Why is divorce such an important factor? Feelings of acute abandonment are typical of children of divorced or separated parents, and such feelings, if left untreated, can lead to depression.

Violence

More and more children are being faced with the stresses of television violence, family violence, and violence in the world, including at school. Some sources say that children exposed to neglect are much more likely to become violent adults.

Poverty

One in four children is born into poverty in the United States (Children's Defense Fund 2000). In poverty, not only are the basic needs of food, clothing, and shelter compromised, but poor children often miss out on important early-education and social opportunities that would lay the groundwork for healthy development.

Basic Brain Chemistry

At birth, an infant's brain contains one hundred billion nerve cells. With the right amount of emotional stimulation, these nerve cells, or neurons, will grow and connect with the various systems in the body that foster functions like seeing, hearing, moving, and expressing thoughts and emotions. A child's brain grows and develops most rapidly between birth and age three.

Infants whose physical and emotional needs go unmet or are inadequately met can develop a condition called failure-to-thrive syndrome. Babies suffer from this syndrome when their needs for human love and care go largely or completely unmet or are severely compromised. Touch, eye contact, and voice contact from caregivers stimulate growth and development in an infant's brain and nervous system. When there is a lack of stimulation, a lack of growth occurs. In extreme cases of failure-to-thrive syndrome, the lack of touch, eye contact, and talking by the caregiver can be fatal to the baby.

Infants and young children who experience a great deal of stress and trauma in their early lives manufacture an excessive amount of the stress hormone cortisol, which can wreak havoc on developing neuronal pathways. Neurons that are responsible for language development and other essential functions may not develop at all or may be unable to communicate with the network of existing neurons. Excessive stress creates greater vulnerability to childhood depression and other social and emotional problems.

Babies thrive when they are held, talked to, and played with by an affectionate caregiver or parent. These interactions, which so many of us take for granted, are the cornerstones of healthy brain development.

Children Grieve Differently Than We Do

Because children's brains are not fully developed, their grieving process is naturally different from that of a mature adult. Children express their grief through their behavior and their play much more clearly than they do through their words. Adults rely predominately on words to express their grief and find relief in "talking it out." Like children, adults experience behavioral changes in response to grief, but they are more able to regulate their behavior and notice how it has changed. Children are by nature focused on themselves and do not yet have the mental abilities to stand back and look at themselves with insight. It is up to adults to learn how to read their child's behavior and help him or her interpret it. Here are some of the ways that children's emotional experience differs from adults':

* Children are more emotionally vulnerable than adults are. Children have had less time to develop the complex defense systems that adults create to protect themselves from emotional pain. In general, children have less emotional scar tissue than adults do.

* Children have not learned the coping skills that can ease the impact of loss and grief. This is especially true of younger children. Loss and grief impact children more directly because they do not yet have an emotional cushion in place to protect themselves against psychological pain.

* Children below the age of seven operate using "primary process."

* Children do not edit or filter their experience of the world; they experience their world through their senses.

* Young children say what they think and act far more spontaneously than do most adults. A child's artwork or play has a certain unfettered quality. One sign of a grieving child is an absence of this free and spontaneous quality in his or her play.

Children Experience Grief:	**Adults Experience Grief:**
* through the symbolic world of play	* by experience of how they have coped with grief in the past
* through their five senses	* by complex intellectual process—the stages described by Elisabeth Kübler-Ross (1969): denial, bargaining, sadness, anger, acceptance

* through their actions or behavior

* by talking it out

* by using mechanisms from childhood such as symbols and ritual to resolve their feelings of grief

Grief and Its Impact on Your Child's Development

In ski racing, the skier must tag each flagged gate in order to finish the course. Similarly, children are continually faced with the need to master new developmental tasks, or milestones, as they grow on their way to adulthood. Some examples of developmental milestones are learning to sit up, learning to crawl, learning to walk, and learning to talk. Each developmental "gate" must be entered and mastered, before the child can move on to the next one. A child does not learn logical thinking without first mastering language. A child does not run before he can walk, nor does he play with peers before he learns how to interact with his parents.

When a significant loss occurs at a critical juncture in development, the child is actually shouldering two tasks: acquiring the skill set that goes with that particular developmental stage, and learning how to cope with loss and grief.

An example of how loss affects development is three-year-old Carrie's story. Carrie was just beginning to develop greater mastery of language when her parents suddenly separated. Carrie was distraught over the changes in her life caused by her parent's breakup, and her command of language began to backslide. The emotional energy Carrie was investing in grieving took away from the energy required to focus on language development. As Carrie adjusted to the loss of her parents' marriage her use of language blossomed again.

For children, who do best in a consistent and nurturing environment, loss and its attendant feeling of grief create an uncomfortable level of stress. Children have to find ways, mostly by trial and error, and by learning from the guidance of adults, how to integrate loss into their existing world. For some, this can be like trying to fit a square peg into a round hole. While a child is working through a loss, her developmental work is put on hold.

Jane's Story: Working through the Loss of a Pet

Jane, four years old, attended preschool three mornings a week and was just beginning to form relationships with the other children in her class, an important developmental social milestone for a child this age. Jane's language skills were developing rapidly and she had begun to stay dry at night. Then Jane's lifetime friend, her pet cat, was hit by a car and killed. Jane was extremely attached to her cat and was inconsolable upon hearing that her cat was dead.

Dealing with the death of her cat temporarily arrested Jane's development. In fact, as is typical of a child's response to loss, Jane began to regress, or go back to earlier developmental stages. She withdrew from friends at school, preferring the company of her parents. She also started using more primitive language and began to wet her bed at night again. When Jane played in the dollhouse in the therapy office, she would collect several miniature cats and place them on the dollhouse beds. She selected a girl doll, which represented Jane, and made her have conversations with the cats and play with them. At times, Jane would get distracted in this symbolic play and the doll would leave the house to play outside. When Jane had the doll return to the house, she would gasp and say, "The door was open!"

As Jane was given permission to do her grief work, her behavior normalized and she quickly got back on developmental track.

What Is Jane Trying to Say through Her Play?

For Jane, working out her grief involved sorting out her feelings of guilt and sadness through playing with her dollhouse. It became evident in her dollhouse play that she felt responsible for leaving the door to the house open, enabling her cat to escape, run into the road, and get hit by a car.

Once Jane's parents observed her playing out this scenario, they were able to reassure her that it wasn't her fault that the cat had died. The cat had been let out many times by many family members and had not died. This death was purely accidental. Four-year-olds are particularly attuned to the relationship between cause and effect, and it took some time for Jane to see that her actions did not cause the cat's death.

A Child's Cycle of Grief

Children will grieve differently depending on their temperament, their developmental level, and external factors such as their level of bonding with their parents.

As I mentioned in chapter 1, your child's grief process may follow the cyclical pattern of protest, pain, and hope.

These three characteristics of childhood grief do not proceed in a neat, linear fashion; instead they may occur out of order, or cycle through in a revolving sequence until hope is the most enduring and prominent feature.

Protest

In this stage, your child may act as if nothing unusual has happened. He may even come across as uncaring and unfeeling. Remember that he is protecting himself from inevitable pain. This is a normal response to grief, similar to an adult's response of denial. A child will want to tell himself that "this didn't really happen." In fact, he will most likely argue with you that it didn't happen. He may ask for concrete, physical evidence of the loss that he can see, touch or feel, though it is not always possible or appropriate to show your child this kind of "proof of death."

Your child may insist that he saw the deceased dog on the street. "But, Mom, it looked just like Scottie," he will protest. Protest is a powerful defense mechanism against feeling pain.

Pain

Try as they might to persuade you that the loss means nothing to them, eventually most children will show signs of emotional pain. Feelings of anger are most often overlooked in a child's grief process, but they are just as important as the feelings of sadness that we tend to associate with grief. Anger is a secondary emotion, that is, there is always another emotion that precedes it such as sadness, disappointment, or frustration. When something is taken away from us, it is natural to feel angry.

It is important that you let your child experience all of her feelings. If a child is given the message that some feelings are okay and some are not okay, she will develop a poor self-image.

You don't need to tolerate inappropriate displays of anger, such as kicking the dog because she didn't get invited to a birthday party and is feeling left out. But you can validate the fact that she feels angry and that beneath that anger there is sadness.

Hope

The saying "Hope springs eternal" is a good one to keep in mind when dealing with your own and your child's feelings of grief around a loss. The process that takes your child from pain to protest to pain to hope to protest and back again may seem to last a very long time. Hope may seem like some elusive light at the end of the tunnel. But don't despair. Children are resilient and most, with help and support from loving parents, will come out on the side of hope.

Hope is not wishful thinking, but a natural human emotion. When children are in the throes of protest and pain, they will feel hopeless. They feel as if suddenly their world has been turned upside down and hope has vanished. Young children are especially sensitive to abandonment and every loss feels like an abandonment of some kind. Whether it's being left out of the most popular group at school or experiencing the death of a parent, the primal fear of abandonment is at the root of all grief over loss.

It may be helpful to remind your child that his feelings are like a bank of clouds and that hope is like the sun hiding behind those dark clouds. For the child who associates loss with darkness, you can explain hope by turning on a light switch in a darkened room. It is a part of our biological makeup—a survival instinct—to move out of emotionally uncomfortable places and into places of hope and renewal.

3

First Feelings,
First Losses

One of the first things an infant learns when he comes into the world is trust—trust that he will be fed when hungry, wrapped in warm blankets when cold, held and soothed when frightened, and loved just for being.

Trust is the first developmental milestone that infants must experience in order to move on to other developmental tasks. Raising a child without trust is like building a house on a foundation of clay.

The Relationship between Trust and Attachment

Trust is built when parents consistently respond to their infant's needs. In order to respond, parents must recognize the cues that their babies are giving them. For example, most parents learn that a certain cry means their baby is hungry; they get to recognize when their baby is ready for a nap. Infants need quick responses from their parents to have their needs for both physical survival and social/emotional development satisfied. If a baby's needs go unmet, she learns that she can't count on people to take care of her and foster her well-being.

This process of reading your baby's cues is known as bonding. Attachment is what happens through the process of bonding. Attachment is that connected feeling between parent and child. There are healthy attachments and unhealthy attachments, or secure and insecure attachments.

When infants experience consistent and reliable responses to their basic needs from their parents, they feel physically and emotionally secure in their relationship. When bonding does not occur or is interrupted because of trauma, neglect, abuse, poverty, or other factors, the child feels insecure and unsure of a safe place in the world.

A child with an unhealthy parental attachment is like a moth drawn to a candle flame. Even an abused child will try and try to please his parents and will have an attachment, though unhealthy, to his parents. He will be instinctively drawn to their caregivers, always hoping that his needs for love and physical well-being will be met, but he will often get burned. The child in this situation learns that other people are not to be trusted and that he needs to rely on himself.

Securely Attached Children Are Resilient

Children who are securely attached to their parents are more resilient than their insecurely attached peers when they experience loss and grief. A secure attachment is one that is marked by a consistently responsive parent who is attuned to his or her child's needs. An insecure attachment is marked by a parent who inconsistently or inadequately meets his or her child's needs. Just as a snugly moored ship is more likely to weather a storm, a securely attached child is better able to withstand the stress that goes along with loss. Securely attached children are less likely to find their grief turning into depression. They bounce back more quickly after a significant loss.

Children who are insecurely attached experience inconsistent parenting marked by periods of neglect and lack of satisfaction of their needs. While most children, when they are feeling shy, overwhelmed, tired, or hungry, can be withdrawn, cranky, or whiny at times, insecurely attached children demonstrate these behaviors consistently and to such a degree that they interfere with their daily functioning. Children who suffer from insecure attachments often have a history of abuse, neglect, exposure to domestic violence, and/or multiple out-of-home placements (e.g., foster care). They are left in a constant state of longing. Insecurely attached children often miss out on the critical window of bonding that occurs during the first few days and months of life. They are mistrustful of relationships. They have learned that they can't count on others to meet their needs and often become sullen and withdrawn or, conversely, excessively whiny and cranky. These children do not have a firm foundation to absorb the shock of loss. Insecurely attached children are more likely to become depressed than successfully grieve through a loss.

But when the parent-child relationship is healthy and strong, you can think of attachment, loss, and grief as a triangle. Attachment is the base, solid and secure. Parent-child attachment only gets stronger as the years go by. Loss comes up one side of the triangle and grief down the other. Think of loss as a dotted line—it won't last. Attachment is a solid line, and grief is a moving line that becomes shorter as it moves toward the security of the parent-child bond.

First Losses

Loss is a natural part of life. Loss is guaranteed to occur at many points and to various degrees throughout the human life cycle. Some psychologists say that loss begins at birth. As soon as the umbilical cord is cut, the infant begins a journey toward individuation, or separateness from her parents. But this need not be seen as a sad process. In fact, it is a joy to see our children grow and evolve into strong and independent adults. Each developmental stage brings new delights and challenges. What parent hasn't celebrated the day they change their child's last soiled diaper?

Each and every developmental stage brings with it a sense of loss for what has gone before and hope for what is to come. Parents look back fondly at how sweet and innocent their baby was but are relieved when their baby starts to sleep through the night. Parents anxiously await their child's first steps but later miss the days when their baby needed to be carried everywhere. The baby who turns into a defiant toddler, whose vocabulary seems to consist only of the word "no," is also a delight when he starts learning how to use the bathroom.

Regression

Children often show their sense of loss by temporarily regressing. Regression is when a child goes back to the behaviors of an earlier developmental stage. Since growth is a two-steps-forward, one-step-backward kind of dance, a certain amount of regression is normal and to be expected. However, loss triggers more than the usual amount of regressive behavior in children. It is often alarming to parents when their toilet-trained child starts having accidents, or when their normally articulate child begins to have trouble finding words, during times of loss and grief. But these regressive behaviors are generally short-lived and resolve on their own in a supportive environment filled with unconditional parental love and acceptance.

Danny's Story: Regression

Four-year-old Danny, whose parents were divorcing, uncharacteristically began to throw tantrums and would demand that he be allowed to drink from a baby bottle again. Danny's parents were surprised at their son's behavior, given the fact that he had prided himself on being a "big boy," putting on his own shoes and getting his own juice from the refrigerator. They wondered if they should give in to Danny's pleas for his bottle.

Danny's parents decided to set boundaries around Danny's demands for a baby bottle. They recognized his need for extra comfort from the bottle, but instead they agreed to meet Danny's needs for soothing in other ways. Danny's father cuddled with his son more often and read him extra stories. Danny's mother made a batch of modeling clay in her son's favorite color, green, and scented it with mint. Within a few days, Danny's behavior normalized to the point where he was no longer demanding bottles.

What Is Danny Trying to Say through His Behavior?

It is often helpful to try to translate your child's behavior into words. What would Danny actually say if he could articulate his feelings? He would probably say something like "I'm so upset by your divorce that I need my bottle again. So give it to me now!" With his behavior, Danny was telling his parents that he couldn't tolerate his own feelings of insecurity around their divorce and was going back to a stage where he received more comfort and soothing from others.

While it is common for parents to worry that their child will remain in a regressed state forever, these worries are usually unfounded. I do not advocate giving into tantrums or encouraging and reinforcing regressive behaviors, but I believe that children, who do not have an adult's coping skills, will not be harmed by spending a limited time in an earlier developmental comfort zone. Children naturally want to grow and mature. To remain in a regressed stage would create guilt and shame for them. It is important for parents to honor their child's needs and also to help them find an alternative means of coping with feelings of loss.

What to Do When Your Child Regresses

Trust what you know to be true about your child. You are the person who knows her best and understands what is best for her. Know that if you continue to provide unconditional support and love, she will come out of her regression in time. Below is some additional advice to keep in mind when your child regresses.

Follow Your Instincts

Children experiencing true loss and grief do not have the emotional energy to manipulate you. Their needs and feelings are genuine and may include reliance on formerly discarded comfort objects. My general advice is to respect your child's needs but also follow your instincts. You probably wouldn't want to give your nine-year-old a baby bottle (and it is unlikely that she would even ask for one). Remain compassionate, and do what feels right to you.

Comfort Your Child

Do comfort your child. Give him plenty of positive one-on-one attention—read stories, sing, draw, and play together. Let him talk about the loss if he wants to, but don't force it. Be a calm, reassuring presence.

Model Taking Care of Yourself for Your Child

Give your child opportunities to self-soothe. Self-soothing, or self-comfort, is what we, as adults, refer to as "taking care of ourselves." Self-soothing involves just that—finding ways to comfort ourselves. This is a learned skill that is best communicated by modeling. Maybe it is music that helps relieve your pain and stress of grieving. Or maybe it is drawing, or talking to a friend, or a hot bubble bath. If you show your child that you take care of yourself, she will feel freer to self-soothe. For a child, play and the expressive arts are wonderful media for helping her to self-soothe and heal during periods of loss and grief. In part 2 of this book, you will be introduced to specific play and art techniques that have helped many children in their healing process.

Other Things to Remember When Your Child Regresses

1. A child's worst fear is the loss of a primary or secondary relationship.

2. Any type of loss can trigger a child's fears of losing the parent.

3. Your child needs extra soothing during times of loss to reassure him that you are not going anywhere and are there for him.

4. Understand that your child does not have the same coping skills that you have.

5. Understand that your child counts largely on tangible, sensory experience for reassurance. Touch, cuddling, and using of security blankets or comfort objects such as stuffed animals and dolls are most appropriate at times of loss.

6. Respect your child's feelings—all of them. Feelings of loss do not only mean sadness but can include anger, betrayal, and guilt, among others.

7. Give your child what she needs, within reason.

Sarah's Story: A Natural Disaster

Natural phenomena such as earthquakes and floods are events that often take people and things away from children and threaten their feeling of security in the world. When an earthquake of sizable magnitude shook Seattle, I received many phone calls from parents concerned about their child's emotional well-being. The question I heard most often from parents after the Seattle-area earthquake was: "My child wants to sleep with us in our bed. Do you think I should let her?"

Eight-year-old Sarah's parents explained that their daughter, who normally fell asleep "the minute her head hit the pillow," was having trouble getting to sleep and staying asleep. Three nights in a row she had lain awake for hours, only to fall asleep briefly and then beg to crawl in with her parents. At first her parents took her back to her own bed, but on the third night her anxiety was so high that they squeezed her in, and she slept peacefully through the night. After two nights, Sarah declared that she wanted to sleep in her own bed again.

What Is Sarah Trying to Say through Her Behavior?

After an extra dose of parent-child contact such as she had when she was an infant and shared the family bed, Sarah was able to overcome her fears of losing her parents in another earthquake and return to her own bed. Like Danny, Sarah was seeking ways to comfort herself. Clearly, Sarah was deeply distressed and needed her parents' help and permission to temporarily regress. When she learned that she had this option, she exercised it just twice and was then empowered to sleep alone again.

Anxiety and Loss

Anxiety can wear the body down and render a child feeling helpless and out of control—both hallmarks of depression. Anxious children are more vulnerable to depression. At a certain point the anxiety becomes too much for the body and mind to handle; the child feels hopeless and emotionally exhausted, which can lead to a depressive episode.

Kyle's Story: Grief Triggered by a Traumatic Event

After the terrorist attacks on the World Trade Center, a young boy was referred to me for symptoms of anxiety. Fearing that his own house would be bombed, Kyle, age seven, began to lose sleep and stop eating. Every little sound made him jumpy. Kyle was convinced that every time a plane flew overhead it was on a direct collision course for his home. Kyle would cower and hide under his bed at the first rumble of a plane's engines.

Soon Kyle's behavior generalized, or spread, to other areas of his life. He began to jump when the phone rang and would startle when he heard his mother start up her car engine in the morning to go to work.

Kyle's anxiety triggered by this terrible event soon gave way to a deep and pervasive fear that he and his family would be killed by a plane crashing into their house.

What Is Kyle Trying to Say through His Play?

When Kyle came to my office for play therapy, he gravitated toward the building blocks. After constructing a tall tower of blocks, Kyle proceeded to knock the tower to the ground by flying a toy plane into it. In this way, Kyle was in charge of what was happening in his world.

Kyle was symbolically playing out the actual disaster that had occurred and providing damage control by instantly mobilizing toy ambulances and police cars to the scene.

Soon Kyle replaced the block tower with a replica of a small house. Try as he might, he was unable to fly the plane into the house.

At age seven, Kyle had a good command of logical thinking and could see that what had happened to the towers was very unlikely to happen to his home. He gave up trying to destroy the house and was able to verbalize his understanding of the situation by saying, "The planes are not coming to my house."

How Do I Know if My Child Is Too Anxious?

Anxiety, grief, and depression are closely related and often occur together. Because their symptoms are so similar, they are easily mistaken for each other. It can be difficult to find the cause of a person's anxiety, especially in children, where we rely heavily on behavioral cues to tell us what is going on in their inner world. Play can help us understand the child's world and respond accordingly to their symbolic communication patterns.

So what is anxiety? We are all familiar with the anticipatory anxiety that comes before making a speech, or getting married, or letting our teenager take out the family car for the first time. Some of the physical signs that tell us we are stressed out or anxious are:

* a higher-than-normal heart rate

* sweaty palms

* muscle tension

* stomach upset

* increased blood pressure

* feelings of dizziness as blood flow is reduced to our brain

It is a normal to feel stress as a part of life. In fact, some stress is a good thing, because it can help keep us aware and motivated to try new things and accomplish them.

All new experiences are typically a bit frightening to one degree or another. For children, who are constantly exposed to new challenges and experiences, this is especially true. Think of all the things children have to learn—speaking, walking, using the toilet, making friends, going to school, learning new sports and academic skills, playing an instrument, etc. The list goes on and on.

Anxiety Disorders

When children become overloaded with too many new experiences or overwhelmed by a traumatic event, such as the death of a parent, they can develop an anxiety disorder.

There are many types of anxiety disorders, but what they all have in common is a persistent and frequent presentation of a pattern of behavior and feelings. Panic, obsessive and compulsive behaviors, phobias, stress after trauma, and school and social phobias are all examples of anxiety problems in children. Any one of these anxiety problems can occur after a loss or death.

For example, a child whose father has died may suddenly resist attending school. If the child's father died while she was at school, she may develop a fear that another close relative will die while she is at school.

In general, if you notice a significant change in your child's eating and sleeping patterns over a two-week period and if he or she complains of stomachaches and headaches, I would recommend consulting your pediatrician. Watch for the following specific symptoms of ongoing anxiety:

* restlessness or being keyed up

* excessive tiredness

* trouble thinking or concentrating

* irritability

* muscle tension

* physical complaints such as stomachaches or headaches

* avoidance behavior—fear and avoidance of situations that were not scary in the past

You will notice that many of these signs and symptoms of anxiety are the same as those listed for depression (see page 47). These two types of mood problems do sometimes overlap. Although most children are resilient and can get past their feelings of anxiety and sadness with the help of their parents and families, it is not unusual for a child to need some extra help at times of loss and grief. Don't hesitate to contact a professional if you have any concerns about your child's mental health.

A Child Life Changes Checklist

The following is a list of life changes that can trigger loss and grief in your child. The list is not all-inclusive. I have left room for you to add your own life events that you feel may trigger grief or anxiety in your child.

For some children, a single event such as moving into a new house will cause sufficient upheaval to create grieving. For other children a move to a new house may be exciting and will not carry with it feelings of profound loss. Some children are particularly sensitive to a particular change. Other children only begin to show signs of grief when life changes add up and become more than they can juggle at one time.

This checklist is not a diagnostic instrument. It is a tool designed to open up your awareness of possible grief triggers for your child. The items are not arranged in order of importance, since each child responds differently to different events or changes.

Instructions: Put a checkmark next to the circumstance that most closely matches your child's current life change. Then go back and put an X next to the circumstances that have affected your child significantly in the past. Write in any events you would like to add to the list.

- ☐ Divorce or separation of parents

- ☐ Introduction of a stepparent

- ☐ New sibling being introduced into the home

- ☐ Extended vacation with one parent

- ☐ Moving to a new residence

- ☐ Going to summer camp

- ☐ Sibling leaving home

- ☐ Death of a parent

- ☐ Death of a grandparent

- ☐ Death of a pet

- ☐ Death of a friend or schoolmate

- ☐ Illness of a loved one

- ☐ Hospitalization of the child or a loved one

- ☐ Starting a new school

- ☐ Being teased or bullied

- ☐ Being rejected by peers

- ☐ Failing in school

- ☐ Losing a home to fire or natural disaster

□ Neglect or abuse

□ _____

□ _____

□ _____

You can use this checklist from time to time to take a reading on the changes your child may be experiencing and to determine how they may or may not be affecting the child's emotional well-being.

Why Is My Child Fine at School but a Real Challenge at Home?

As a child and family therapist, I hear parents say that their child is an angel at school, but at home the child flexes his muscles, and talks back, and challenges the parent on *every* conceivable level. This is actually a good thing, I tell parents. "It means that the child feels safe and secure enough around the parents to express his or her ever-changing emotional world." This does not mean that as parents we need to take everything our children dish out. Instead, we can set limits and provide structure in a nurturing way so that the child can learn appropriate ways of expressing him- or herself.

Children Express Themselves Through . . .

* action more than words

* symbolic play

* their five senses

* physical signs (headaches, stomachaches, etc.)

Please use the following exercise to help you understand your child's way of coping with challenging situations. A journal or notebook is a good place to record your answers. You can do this exercise every few months to see how your child's coping skills change.

How Does Your Child Express Himself?

Actions/Behaviors:

Feeling-Behavior Patterns Typical for Your Child:

When my child is angry, he _____ .

When my child is sad, he _____ .

When my child is frustrated, he _____ .

When my child is happy, he _____ .

When my child experienced the loss/death of _____ , he

_____ .

Symbolic Play:

My child usually likes to play _____ .

What patterns or themes have I noticed in my child's day- to-day play? _____

Since the loss/death of _____ , my child now plays

_____ .

What patterns or themes, if any, have changed since the loss?

_____

The Five Senses

Touch:

Describe your child's level of comfort with touch. Does he like to be held or not? Does he enjoy cuddling with familiar people and animals? Has there been an experience in his life that has changed how he feels about touch? Note your thoughts below:

Sight:

Does your child learn well by looking at pictures and books? Does your child mostly take in their world by what they see? Describe:

Sound:

Is your child particularly attuned to sound? Does she learn best by listening? Does she especially enjoy music?

Taste:

Does your child like a variety of foods? Does he wonder what things taste like? Does he tend to comfort himself with food or does he reject food when he is upset?

Smell:

Does your child stop to "smell the roses"? Does she enjoy the aroma of scented candles or clay? Does she associate memories with smells? Describe:

What Works Best:

What sensory stimulation is most helpful in soothing your child during times of grief? Is music helpful? How about a warm glass of milk before bed, a warm bath, extra hugs, or cuddling with a favorite stuffed animal?

Physical Signs:

The Body-Mind Connection

Does your child tend to experience physical pains like stomach-aches, headaches, or general malaise when he is emotionally upset?

When my child experienced the loss/death of _____ , he or she complained of the following physical hurts: _____

_____

_____

_____

List what helped your child feel better:

_____

4

The Difference Between Grief and Depression

Grief is a natural process that is fluid rather than rigid or static. Children who are grieving freely express anger, sadness, disappointment, betrayal, and frustration, among other emotions. Children and adults experience feelings in a cyclical rather than linear pattern until the feelings are resolved. Resolution occurs when the child makes some sense of the external loss and can integrate it into his or her internal world. In essence, the child finds a way to get some meaning out of what has occurred and, with this newfound meaning, move on with his or her life.

Children at different developmental stages will ascribe different meanings to loss and grief. For example, a three-year-old will believe that the loss is impermanent and do all kinds of mental gymnastics to persuade herself that her beloved grandmother is alive and well when in actuality she is dead.

To an eight-year-old, seeing is believing. Children of this age prefer to see concrete, physical evidence that loss or death has occurred but, when this is not possible, they are able to use logical thinking to understand the death or loss in physical terms—the deceased no longer breathes or eats or moves.

It is important that parents or other trusted adults provide stability and act as a safe container for a child's feelings of grief. Consider how vast and confusing the world would be if we adults did not have structure, routine, and consistency in our lives. To a vulnerable child this is even more important. Parents can help their child grieve by providing a stable environment with boundaries in which the child can feel safe to express all that he or she is feeling.

Depression

Think of grief as a fluid process—we move through a loss. Depression is grief that has become stuck. When children have difficulty expressing their feelings around loss or death, those feelings remain ungrieved and block normal development until they are expressed. Many adults carry ungrieved losses from childhood and suffer from depression and anxiety disorders. Grief is actually a preventive mechanism that keeps us from getting depressed. If we are aware of what we are feeling and can identify what has triggered that feeling, then we are well on our way to healing.

Most people, when asked how they are feeling, don't really know. Feelings change rapidly and it is even possible to have more than one feeling at once. As some research shows, we can have up to sixty feelings in one minute. That's one feeling every second!

The first step in helping your child grieve through a loss is to identify as closely as possible what he or she is feeling. Secondly, you'll need to find out what specific event or events have triggered this feeling. The play exercises in chapters 11 and 12 will help you to help your child identify his or her feelings and the triggering event that have led to the feelings.

Below are a few facts and figures related to depression in childhood.

* Divorce remains the leading cause of childhood depression.

* One or more significant life changes, such as a move to a new area, a change of schools, or the death of a parent or grandparent, can trigger a major depressive episode in a child.

* The American Academy of Child and Adolescent Psychiatry reports that as many as 5 percent of all children in the

United States, or 3.4 million children, experience one or more episodes of clinical depression during childhood.

* Children are becoming depressed at earlier ages.

* Once a child experiences an episode of depression, he or she is more vulnerable to subsequent depressive episodes.

How Do I Know If My Child Is Depressed?

If you observe five or more of the symptoms below in your child for more than two weeks, it is likely that your child is depressed and needs professional help.

You know your child best. If you have any concerns about his response to a loss or major life change, consult a professional. Don't wait. In fact, if your child's functioning is affected, if he stops wanting to go to school, or if he exhibits any one of the symptoms so much that it significantly disrupts his life for a two-week period, then I suggest that you seek professional help.

The Signs and Symptoms of Childhood Depression

* A down mood for most of the day; a pervasive "I don't care what happens" attitude

* A lack of interest in activities your child used to enjoy

* Significant weight gain or loss

* Sleeping a lot more or a lot less

* Significant increase or decrease in activity

* Complaints of exhaustion and overtiredness almost every day

* Feelings of worthlessness or low self-esteem (your child no longer seems to care about or value herself—life seems meaningless)

* Difficulty concentrating and thinking, focusing on school-work, reading, making decisions, or solving problems

* Recurrent thoughts of death

* **Suicidal thoughts or gestures: If your child talks about suicide, SEEK PROFESSIONAL HELP IMMEDIATELY. Take all suicidal threats and talk seriously. "I want to kill myself" is an example of a comment that must be taken seriously.**

Causes of Childhood Depression

Childhood depression can stem from psychological or biological factors, or some combination of these. Psychological causes of childhood depression relate to negative thought patterns and ungrieved losses. Biological causes relate to chemical imbalances in the brain. It is increasingly believed that thoughts and feelings affect brain chemistry. Below are some of the common roots of depression in children.

* Ungrieved loss—a loss that doesn't get talked about or "worked out"

* A chemical imbalance in the brain (low levels of serotonin, a neurotransmitter in the brain has been identified in childhood and adult depression)

* Negative self-talk (e.g., "I am a bad person")

* Unexpressed anger that is turned inward ("I hate myself. I am to blame"); a general state of emotionally beating up on oneself

* A combination of some or all of these factors

The Fine Line between Grief and Depression

In general when a child is depressed he presents with a feeling of helplessness or loss of control of life events—things just keep happening and problems keep piling up until the child feels he cannot dig himself out.

If your child is grieving but not depressed, he has a sense of resiliency or strength that makes him want to pull out of the sadness or anger. He shows a degree of energy and motivation to get better. He may be overwhelmed with emotion, but these emotions get smaller rather than bigger over time. The child is also able to accept comfort from you and also able to comfort himself.

Read about Camille and Jackson below. Three-year-old Camille, whose grandfather died, is an example of a grieving child. Eight-year-old Jackson, whose parents divorced, is an example of a depressed child.

Camille's Story: Grieving the Death of Her Grandfather

Camille's parents brought her to me for assessment when she began to cry herself to sleep at night after her grandfather died. While they provided a safe, stable home environment and validated Camille's experience of the loss of her grandfather by allowing her to express her feelings, they wanted to be sure that Camille would recover from this first loss in her young life.

Camille seemed to be her happy-go-lucky self during the day, but most nights she wanted to sleep with her parents and would be inconsolable a few nights a week. Camille expected that her grandfather would come back, and her parents wondered if this was a normal thought process for a three-year-old.

Camille did not present as a depressed child. Although she was sad some of the time and more irritable than usual, she was mostly upbeat and had not lost interest in activities that she enjoyed. She still had fun at her ballet class, continued to attend preschool, and was eating well, although her sleep patterns were somewhat disrupted.

What Is Camille Trying to Say through Her Play?

My observation of Camille at play clued me in to her ability to work through her grieving process, with the assistance of her parents. During a few short observations, I learned that Camille was able to act out and to some degree verbalize her feelings as she narrated her fantasy play.

Camille would join her grandfather doll and grandmother doll in an embrace, saying, "I love you, Grandpa," mimicking her grandmother's voice. It was clear to me that Camille felt that her grandfather was still loved and cared for by his wife.

Play Interventions to Use at Home

I suggested that Camille's parents try the following play activities at home. These are just a sampling of some of the activities that you can do with your own child at home. Many more are presented in part 2 of this book. The exercises are designed to be simple but effective. Materials can be found around the house or purchased inexpensively.

Exercise: Drawing Out the Pain

This exercise is designed to connect the body with the mind through the act of drawing or scribbling. Often, emotions that are stuck in a child's mind may be released more easily through drawing and scribbling than through talking.

Materials:

Paper and markers or crayons

Directions:

Use a large piece of paper such as a sheet of butcher paper, or use a paper grocery bag, cutting the paper into a long rectangle. Tape the paper securely to a hard, flat surface such as the floor or a table.

Let your child choose markers and/or crayons to draw with and ask him to scribble on the paper. Encourage him to use different colors to express different feelings. Red could be anger; blue could represent sadness. The idea is to get rid of the chaotic feelings around the loss. This can be quite an invigorating activity for the child as he tries to cover the whole paper and get all of his feelings out. When he is done, ask him if he would like to tell you about his drawing or scribble. Ask him how he is feeling. Many children will answer, "Tired," or "Better," or "I don't know." Avoid making judgments or asking too many questions. Let your child decide if he wants to keep the paper or throw it away. Some children feel that the act of throwing the paper away will get rid of the feelings; however, feelings will likely remain for a time.

Exercise: Magic Wand, Magic Wand, Make the Yucky Feelings Disappear

As long as it doesn't interfere with your religious or cultural beliefs, "magic" is okay to use with young children—most of them believe in it and young children thrive on fantasy. Magical fantasies are not a means for escape, but a developmental coping mechanism. The power of suggestion can be incredibly powerful in healing or physical complaints.

Materials:

Cardboard or stiff paper; glitter and glue (Alternatively, purchase an inexpensive water and glitter-filled cylinder available at most toy stores for under $5).

Directions:

If you are making your own magic wand, cut a wand shape out of the cardboard and decorate it with glue and glitter. Next, make up some magical words, or use old standards like "abracadabra." Tell your child that this magic wand is special and will make those yucky feelings go away. Wave the wand over your child's stomach (or head or heart—wherever the hurt is) and say, "Magic wand, magic wand, make Camille's stomachache be gone. Abracadabra, ala kazam!"

Jackson's Story: Working through Depression

Eight-year-old Jackson had a rocky history. Before coming to live with his now-divorced adoptive parents, he had lived in five different foster homes. After the divorce, the court awarded Jackson's mother primary custody of her son with alternate weekend visits with his father.

Jackson's father was an authoritarian parent who would not allow Jackson to cry or express any grief over the divorce in his presence. Jackson's mother was overly permissive and allowed Jackson to draw on the walls when he was angry and eat whatever he wanted—mostly junk food.

Because of his many moves, Jackson had been unable to form lasting peer relationships essential to his developmental age. Chronologically, Jackson may have been eight years old, but I estimated his emotional age to be that of a six-year-old.

The divorce of his parents was the last straw for Jackson. He was ill-equipped to deal with this loss on top of the many other ungrieved losses he had suffered.

Jackson presented as a depressed child. He had lost interest in playing baseball, his favorite game; he had nightmares frequently; he had lost two pounds in two weeks; and he was having trouble concentrating on his schoolwork. His mood was one of sadness and irritability almost every day during a two-week period.

What Is Jackson Trying to Say through His Play?

It was watching Jackson's play, or his lack thereof, that let me know how deeply this child was hurting: his clenching and dropping of sand from the sand-play table, as if the very essence of his life were slipping away; his unwillingness to join me in a board game that his parents had told me he usually loved to play; his flat emotional response, as if nothing mattered; and, finally, his regression—curling up on my beanbag chair with his baby blanket. He would give only one- or two-word answers to my questions. It was as if Jackson barely had the energy to talk.

After six months of weekly therapy, his symptoms showed marked improvement. Jackson exhibited an ability to bounce back once he began to learn to trust and safely express his feelings. His parents, who each had attended parenting classes and learned of the impact their volatile divorce had had on their child, were now equipped to continue helping their son at home.

Exercise: Clay Play

Children who are experiencing the anger and distress that divorce brings up may be especially helped by this exercise. This is an excellent activity to help break up stuck feelings. Working with clay is generally good for children who are experiencing strong emotions such as anger, fear, or sadness.

Materials:

A pack of modeling clay (available at toy or art stores for less than $5). Do not substitute Play-doh, because it is soft and malleable and does not require the kind of focused physical energy that is necessary to help the child work out her stress and anger.

Directions:

Suggest that your child work the clay until it is soft, using hands or elbows. Provide tools like a rubber mallet to pound the clay. Fists also work well. The idea is to help the child to release and express emotion through this simple action, not to make something. Your children may cry or express anger while working with the clay, because once the body starts moving, the emotions start moving.

If your child does want to make something out of the clay, that's great. Let her initiate what it is she wants to make. If she doesn't know what to make you might suggest these things:

* people

* a family

* a self-depiction

* a mask representing her own face

* a planet: Roll one color of clay into a small ball, and then wrap the ball in a layer of another clay color and then

another until you have a large layered ball. For each layer, pound the clay flat so it can be wrapped around the previous layer. When the ball is complete, have the child cut the "planet" in half. She will be amazed to see the colorful layers inside. You can explain that the core is her heart—protected and always there at her center. The layers are emotions like sadness, anger, and hurt, which all have a purpose.

When Play Becomes Aggressive

In part 2, learning how to observe and interpret your child's play will be covered in depth. But now is a good time to say a bit about aggressive play.

A distressed mother once called me and said, "I used the clay-play exercise you suggested at home, and my son built a bird's nest, put tiny clay eggs in it, and then proceeded to smash the whole thing with a rubber mallet."

Understandably it was disturbing for this mother to see her usually peaceful child destroy a bird's nest. My general rule of thumb is that if the child is not directly hurting himself or others, then the play is safe. However, if your child is constantly playing out hostile themes that are disturbing to you and that do not resolve over time, again, do not hesitate to get an opinion from a child mental-health specialist.

It is safe and healthy for children to act out their anger through play. Suppressing anger will only lead to aggression spilling out into other areas of life. Play is an effective way for children to express and release their hurt and anger so they can begin to heal.

Throughout this book we will be talking about other play techniques that you can use to help understand your child's grieving process. When combined with consistency, nurturance, and personal ritual, play can be one of the most helpful—and often overlooked—tools at your disposal!

5

Explaining Death to Your Child: Ages and Stages

Talking about death to a child is a difficult thing to do. We want to shelter our children from frightening and painful aspects of life. We may even have a hard time thinking about death ourselves. But there are ways we can discuss death with our children that will help them understand it, and fear it less.

How to Talk to Your Child about Death

Even though children don't fully develop logical thinking and understand of death as permanent until age seven, it is not too early to begin talking with your child about death when he or she has some proficient mastery of language, at about the age of three for most children. Here are some things to keep in mind when you talk to your child about death:

Use simple, clear, and direct language to explain death.

Four-year-old Ricky, who was told that his grandpa had gone to sleep for a long time and was not going to wake up, started to dread going to sleep at night, fearing that, like his grandpa, he would never wake up.

Six-year-old Cindy, who was told that their family had lost their dog, Sam, when she had actually died, waited expectantly by the phone, believing that someone would find her beloved dog and return her.

Instead, Ricky's and Cindy's parents could have said:

"Ricky, You know that Grandpa has been sick for a long time. Well, he died last night in the hospital. Grandma was with him, holding his hand. I know that you loved him a lot. Do you want to ask me anything? Would you like to play or draw? We can try some activities together to help ourselves feel better."

"This is sad news for me, Cindy, and it may be for you, too. Sam got hit by a car. He's dead. There's nothing we can do to make him come alive again, but we can do some things together to help our sad feelings get better."

Rely on your religious, spiritual, or cultural beliefs.

Almost all cultures and religions include a concept of life going on in some form after death. Many families use the concept of heaven to explain death to children in a gentle and nonjarring way. Heaven symbolizes a peaceful, eternal place that can be conceptualized by the child. However, the idea of heaven does not work for all families or jibe with their religious beliefs.

Some faiths teach that this life is the only one and that death is a final end. Others feature the discrete concepts of heaven and hell, equating heaven with good behavior and hell with bad behavior.

Whatever your family's religious beliefs, use them to help your child understand and cope with grief. Spiritual beliefs are personal and often rooted in a particular religious faith.People's conception of God is individual and there are myriad opinions on how children view God. Every family has their own system of beliefs, which is invaluable in times of loss and grief.

Decide for yourself whether to bring your child to the funeral.

Some parents choose to include children in funerals and memorial services and some do not. Some think that three is too young for participation, but that four is old enough. There are no right or wrong answers. You know your child best and what he or she can and cannot tolerate.

Be clear about your own beliefs and feelings around death.

Are you frightened of death? Do you believe in reincarnation? Do you believe there is life after death or do you believe that death is the end of the road? Children usually develop their own concepts of death based on what their parents believe.

Show your feelings.

Children learn about expressing their feelings from their parents. Early on, children pick up whether it is okay to express their feelings, or whether some feelings are fine while other feelings are not acceptable.

Communicate stability to your child

It is common for children to fear that all of their close relationships are in jeopardy when a beloved person or pet dies. In circumstances where several people who are important to the child die, such as in a natural disaster, it is even more important to assure the child that such an event is very rare and that he or she is safe and will be taken care of.

Mary's Story: Learning that All Feelings Are Okay

Seven-year-old Mary had never seen her mother cry. Every time that Mary cried she felt weak and ashamed. She looked up to her mother and wondered why she couldn't be just like her. When Mary's parents divorced she often felt her eyes welling up with tears. Wasn't her mother upset about this huge disruption in their family life?

Mary's mother had learned from her parents that feelings were meant to be hidden. It wasn't until her daughter became depressed from the energy of trying to hold in all her feelings that she realized what a disservice she was doing to her daughter by not modeling healthy expression of her own feelings. Little by little, Mary's mother became able to risk showing more feelings, and in turn Mary's depression lifted.

What Is Mary Trying to Say through Her Behavior?

By holding in her feelings, Mary was saying that she was ashamed of her feelings. She was afraid that she would disappoint and displease her mother if she showed her true emotions. As Mary's mother modeled showing more of her own feelings, Mary felt more free to express her feelings and her depression lifted.

Sam's Story: Mourning the Loss of a Best Friend and a Grandmother

When nine-year-old Sam's grandmother died and his best friend moved away, he felt that his world had been turned upside down and would never be the same again.

Sam's parents gave him the message that he would get through these painful losses. They communicated this by accepting all of Sam's feelings and reassuring him that painful feelings do change. They told him that he would soon feel better.

To help facilitate Sam's healing, Sam's parents maintained their household routines as much as possible. This stability helped to provide a sense of normalcy for Sam in his otherwise chaotic world.

What Is Sam Trying to Say through His Behavior?

Sam was at a developmental age where friends are of great importance. Having a close friend move away *and* a grandparent die around the same time triggered *extreme* feelings of loss and grief in Sam. In his eyes, the world really had been turned upside down. Chaos reigned. Sam's parents helped him through this difficult time by maintaining as much order and stability as possible.

Learning through Play

Children's play tells us about how they learn about death. In order to understand death, children must first learn about permanence—an object or person doesn't cease to exist just because it's out of view.

Games of peekaboo may be played with babies as early as six months. By two years old, children like to hide from their parents and delight in the game of disappearance they have created. Two-year-olds also like to drop food and cups or bottles from their high-chairs and have their parents retrieve them, only to drop them again! By four and five years old, hide-and-seek is a favorite game. Six-year-olds often experiment with turning all the lights off in their room and seeing how long they can tolerate the darkness. By seven and eight years old, fantasy play involving being grown up and on their own is a favorite; at nine, children may threaten to run away when frustrated or angry with their parents.

All of these childhood games have to do with disappearance and recovery. The lights go off. The lights go on. Children hide and feel a rush of relief when their parents find them. In play, children are at the control switch of their own innate fears of separation and abandonment. They are also learning about loss and death, permanence and impermanence.

I remember when my children were three and five and playing hide-and-seek with a few older neighborhood children who had come across the street to visit. When Tommy, an eight-year-old boy, hid and didn't come out of hiding, my three-year-old son began to cry and my five-year-old daughter showed great signs of distress at Tommy's seemingly permanent disappearance. When Tommy finally emerged from the attic, my kids were full of questions: "Where were you?" "I thought you had gone away forever."

For young children, loss brings up worries about abandonment and rightly so. The child is solely dependent on his or her parents for physical and emotional survival and will be for many years.

Ages and Stages

All children, all over the world, play. How children play varies according to their age, their developmental stage, and their emotional state. A four-year-old child who has endured the trauma of having an absent mother might act more like a three-year-old in play. The play of grieving children, no matter what their age, will most likely differ in theme and content from that of non-grieving children. The play of a grieving child will eventually gravitate to the source or experience of the grief.

Below is an outline of the child's main tasks, concerns, and ways of dealing with loss at various developmental stages.

Two- and Three-Year-Olds

Accomplishment versus failure

Two- and three-year-olds are working on becoming more independent and doing things for themselves. They want to put on their own clothes, tie their own shoes, and get their own juice, but they still need their parents' help to do many of these things. The more independent a toddler feels, the more competent she will feel, paving the way for a strong self-image. A preschooler who has had a positive experience of early bonding will feel confident in venturing out into the world. A preschooler who has had interrupted bonding or inadequate early bonding will be more likely to demonstrate significant signs of distress when separating from the parent.

Temperament

A child's temperament will also affect how he deals with loss and separation. This will be discussed in greater detail in chapter 9. More sensitive, introverted children are more apt to show anxiety with separation regardless of early bonding experiences in contrast to their more outgoing peers.

Three-year-old Carly believed in magic and had a special love for and belief in fairies. When Carly's cat, Smokey, wandered off, she counted on her fairy friends to bring him back. She commanded the fairies to retrieve Smokey from wherever he had gone. However, weeks went by, and Smokey did not come back.

When the cat had been gone for a month, Carly's parents told her he was not likely to return. Even so, Carly believed that Smokey had simply gone away for a while, maybe on a long walk.

Carly was faced with a particular kind of loss, an uncertain loss. No one could be sure that the cat was gone for good, but a month was a long time. Carly's parents remained honest and straightforward with their daughter, using simple language to explain that the cat was either lost and had found a new home or had gone to cat heaven.

Still, Carly was quite adamant that he would return via express delivery by her fairies.

Carly was in a developmental stage where grasping control of the world is extremely important. Death and loss at this age are viewed as reversible. Pets can leave but they will come back, even though they are dead. It is not uncommon for three- and four-year-olds to insist that they have seen their deceased pet on the street or in someone's yard running around. Children of this age will often ask their parents to provide food and water for a person or pet who has died. They will ask questions like "How can Grandma breathe?" In their minds, life goes on and on.

Four-, Five-, and Six-Year-Olds

The drive for independence
Children of this age are busy finding their place in the larger social world that exists outside of the family unit. School, playgroups, religious education classes, and other experiences mark the social development of this age.

Four-, five-, and six-year-olds are learning to cooperate with others and gain better control of their emotions. Tantrums are less frequent as children are more able to regulate their internal world much as a thermostat regulates room temperature.

The importance of language development
Children between the ages of five and six experience a huge surge in the growth of their language skills and most command a ten thousand word vocabulary!

With a greater command of language comes a more clear and realistic perception of death. Four-year-olds may still believe that death is reversible, but they may also begin to test their existing reality through their play by making dolls disappear for longer periods of time or hiding objects in a game of treasure hunt.

Separation
As children get older, they are able to tolerate longer periods of separation from their parents. They have enough experience to know that when their parents leave for work, they will return. They understand that when their parents go out and leave them with a babysitter, they will come back. In cases of neglect when parents are gone for extended periods or do not tell their children when they will be back, fears of abandonment loom large and greatly impact a child's development.

New concepts of death
Five- and six-year-olds ask a lot of questions about death. Just as children this age may become skeptical about the existence of

Santa Claus, they may begin to experiment with the idea that death may be permanent. They may fall back on earlier beliefs that death is reversible, and then allow themselves to consider the possibility that it is not.

Five-year-old Riley's older brother, Kevin, became ill and died. Riley told her mother that Kevin would be back and begged her not to pack up his things and put them away. After several weeks, when Kevin didn't come home, Riley began to ask her mother if her brother might not be coming home.

Riley was taking a great emotional risk in trying out the possibility that Kevin might be "all the way gone." As Riley began to accept the fact that Kevin wouldn't be playing with his toys anymore, she experienced fear and sadness. As she glimpsed the finality of death, she became anxious. The integration of new information into the child's psyche always carries with it a certain amount of anxiety.

For several weeks Riley went back and forth between her ideas about death, finally finding a middle ground in the belief that her brother wasn't coming back but was alive and well in heaven.

Children who are around four to six years old are putting a great deal of energy into their rapid language development and preparing for the transition to logical thinking. And the more sophisticated tools for dealing with grief, including language, are developing but not yet fully present. As a result, understanding death and handling grief can be quite overwhelming for a child of this age.

Knowing something in an intellectual way is different from actually assimilating it into an existing mental framework. It's like trying to change a habit. We may know we need to stop eating butter to lower our cholesterol, but actually doing it is another matter. And think of the anxiety associated with giving up a favorite food. Children are constantly faced with the necessity of trading an old idea in for a new one as their brain develops and matures, which makes grieving even more challenging for them.

Seven-, Eight-, and Nine

The drive toward competence

Children in this age group are highly sensitive to what their friends think of them. This is an age where belonging and being accepted, friendships and social relationships are of vast importance. Whether or not an eight-year-old is invited to a birthday party that "everyone else is going to" can make or break the child's day. Children of this age want to do things right. They have strong feelings about right and wrong and are sticklers for following the rules of games.

As children develop a better sense of themselves they feel more secure in pondering the mysteries of death. They become more sensitive to death in nature, such as the dying of leaves in autumn. Children in this age group often consider the possibility of an afterlife, viewing death in a broader and more realistic way, with less fantasy or magical thinking and a greater acceptance of the inevitability of death.

Fear of death

A child in this age group may exhibit greater fear around death as an unknown and abstract concept. The reality of death can be frightening to children, since it calls up fears of abandonment. "Who will take care of me when I die?" "Does everyone die?" and "What happens when I die?" are all questions that are commonly asked by older children.

The need for accurate language about death

The more accurate and factual information you can give your older child about death, the better he or she will be able to formulate an understanding of death that fits his or her comfort level.

Words like funeral, casket, cremation, and bereavement are appropriate for use when you are explaining death to your child at this age, depending on your personal and/or religious and spiritual views. Older children want to feel well-informed and included. It is often helpful to let children this age attend funerals and memorial services in order for them to gain closure around a death.

Table 1: How Children Perceive Death at Different Ages

Age	Ideas and experience of death
Infancy	Has no cognitive experience of death. Will experience death as an interrupted attachment. Behavior will change.

2 to 3	Sees death as temporary, reversible. Has fantasies of immortality.
4 to 6	Attempts to explain and rationalize death. Experiments through play and actions with the idea that death might be permanent.
7 to 9	Gains ability to reason. Understands logical explanations of death including acceptance of mortality. Understands biological basis of death. Ideas around death are closer to those of an adult.

Complicated Grief

If children are allowed to express their feelings around a loss as it occurs or immediately after it occurs, they are much more likely to heal and move along a steady course of development.

Complicated grief occurs when a child gets stuck somewhere in the grief process. They remain in protest and get increasingly angry or even rageful. Or, they cannot seem to pull themselves out of the pain phase of grief even with the help of their parents. Hope remains distant in the vast ocean of the child's feelings.

Complicated grief takes longer and is harder to heal because it is affected by significant factors such as:

* a parent's unwillingness to validate or respond to a child's repertoire of feelings

* parents who abuse drugs or alcohol

* consistently depressed and emotionally unavailable parents

* more than one significant loss at a time

* a child with developmental delays

* missed developmental stages due to trauma or crisis

* a fragile parent-child bond

* rigid or lax parenting

The number one factor in helping children heal from loss and grief is a responsive, understanding, supportive, and validating parent.

Take Time Out to Explore Your Own Feelings around Loss

It is inevitable that your child's experience of loss and grief will create, to one degree or another, feelings of loss for you, too. I find it helpful to explore my own feelings around loss when helping children cope with their losses.

Discuss these questions with a trusted friend or partner, or write your answers in a journal to help you explore your inner world as it relates to loss.

Exercise: Exploring Your Thoughts and Feelings Around Loss

1. What are your beliefs about death (personal, spiritual, religious)?

2. What are you feeling about this particular loss?

3. What has helped you through your grieving processes in the past (e.g., personal or religious rituals such as lighting candles; saying prayers; commemorating the deceased; or talking to a friend, clergy person, or counselor?

4. How can you use what has helped you to help your child?

During times of grief it's important to take care of ourselves and our families. Some suggestions for family-nurturing activities that parents have found helpful for themselves and their children are:

* Take a hot bubble bath

* Walk with a friend

* Reserve a "family night" once a week—play board games, make popcorn, do something you all enjoy together

* Look at albums of photos of the deceased and talk about his or her life

* Give each other foot rubs

* Treat yourself and your family members to a getaway. This needn't be expensive. Visit a museum or a park that you have never been to. Or, if you can, take a night away in a hotel. Let someone else take care of you.

Everyone has a different way of taking care of themselves when it comes to the pain of loss and grief, but remember this is a time to pay attention to your own needs as well as the needs of your child. Be kind to yourself.

6

Divorce and Other Losses

The first time I saw six-year-old Jamie, he was sitting at the child's table in my waiting room, hunched over a piece of paper with a pencil stub clenched between his fingers. His nails were bitten down to the quick and, although it was unseasonably warm for May, Jamie was wearing a ski coat, zipped up so that it covered the lower half of his face.

Jamie's mother sat leafing through a magazine. Her son had his back turned toward her, his pencil poised in readiness to draw, but when I glanced at his paper I didn't see any marks. I wondered how long Jamie had been holding his pencil in the air, staring into space.

Jamie's mother and I had met a week earlier at her son's intake appointment. Like many parents who are perplexed over a sudden change in their child's behavior, she wanted to understand why her son had changed from an engaging child who enjoyed playing baseball and talked nonstop to a withdrawn and sullen boy.

Jamie's mother was at a loss to explain her son's behavior changes. He poked at his food and had lately turned down a trip to McDonald's. He could never find his baseball glove when it was time for practice. His first-grade teacher had recently written a note home saying that Jamie had hit another boy on the playground over a routine game of four-square. It wasn't until Jamie's mother mentioned that she and her husband had been fighting a great deal lately and were divorcing that I began to fit the pieces of Jamie's behaviors together. Like most well-intentioned parents, Jamie's mother insisted that she and her husband were careful not to fight in front of Jamie and his younger sister. She said, "Jamie doesn't even know we're getting divorced yet."

Why was Jamie acting so differently from his usual behavior while his four-year-old sister continued to maintain a happy-go-lucky attitude? Why had Jamie hit another child, which was so out of character for him? How could his parents' impending divorce be affecting Jamie when his mother was doing her best to protect him from adult problems?

When I said hello to Jamie and introduced myself, he remained motionless in his chair, his fingers tightening around his pencil as if it were his security blanket. Jamie's mother started to apologize for her son's behavior. She turned to me and said, "I'm sorry. He's not usually like this," and then turned to Jamie. "Jamie, say hello, honey."

I said, "It's okay," and gently approached Jamie, kneeling down beside his chair. I told him my name again and invited him to come into my office. With some coaxing from his mother, Jamie got up from the table and, clutching his pencil, followed me into the play therapy room. He sat himself down in my chair and said in a voice muffled by his coat collar, "I don't have to talk to you."

I could tell that Jamie was feeling angry and resistant. I also knew, from his mother, that he cried himself to sleep at night and was usually a charming and bright child. When children grieve, they often take a stance of protest that can range from resistance to anger to outright rage. It was clear that Jamie was using all of his energy to defend himself against painful and frightening feelings. It often feels safer for a child to get in touch with his or her anger than what lies beneath it—sadness. Anger is what's called a secondary emotion, meaning that there is another feeling, such as disappointment, frustration, or sadness, that precedes it.

Jamie had such deep feelings of sadness buried beneath his anger that it took several weeks for me to reach him. As Jamie became more trusting he was able to express his feelings. During play therapy Jamie played mostly at the sand table, filling up and emptying containers of sand. His choice of sensory play seemed to soothe him. The actions of filling and emptying told me that this child was trying to let go of long-held emotions.

After some time Jamie was able to put words to his play and tell me how afraid he felt inside and how "big" his feelings were. By using feeling flashcards to help him identify his feelings, he was able to gain more control of his feelings and begin to heal. Eventually Jamie was able to tell his parents how upset their fighting had made him feel, despite their efforts to shield him from the tensions between them. Jamie has now moved through that difficult period in his life and is a happy, well-adjusted boy.

Divorce as a Trigger to a Child's Grief

Although there are many life events that can trigger grief in children, divorce remains the leading cause of childhood depression. More and more children are subjected to the trauma and loss that come with divorce, and profound loss of this type that is untreated or unaddressed can lead to childhood depression.

Child psychologists, pediatricians, and other professionals involved in children's health and welfare hold different opinions on how much divorce rocks a child's emotional world. But the vast majority of experts believe that divorce wreaks significant emotional havoc for a child. A very few people who deal with children professionally think that divorce does not significantly impact a child. However, even those in this small minority believe that divorce has some negative impact on a child.

I don't recall that I have ever had a parent tell me that divorce didn't have a major impact on his or her child or children for some period of time. However, the degree and duration in which children are impacted varies greatly.

As a stepmother, I am well acquainted with the stress that such a profound change can create for a child and his or her family. My stepson was five when my husband and I married. He is now seventeen and a well-adjusted and emotionally secure individual, but he definitely went through some challenges to get where he is today.

Divorce is not easy for anyone concerned, especially a vulnerable child. However, there are many things that you, as a parent, can do to help your child adjust to a divorce.

Yes, children will most likely go through periods of profound loss and grief around a divorce. The emotional upheaval your child feels is not a onetime event that he or she simply gets over; it is a process, like all grieving. In children, a feeling of loss will reoccur at different developmental ages and stages. Your child will need your help and/or that of a professional to negotiate his or her complex feelings, which can run the gamut from fear to anger to betrayal to guilt and back again.

Divorce is no doubt the most major upheaval that can occur in their lives, barring the death of a parent. But children are more resilient than we think. If divorce is handled thoughtfully by both parents, the emotional fallout for the child is minimized and the adjustment and healing process kicks in more quickly.

Fear of Abandonment

Divorce plays on your child's biggest fear: that he or she will be abandoned by you or your spouse. This fear of abandonment is at the heart of the child's grief over a divorce. Add to a child's fear of abandonment the belief that he or she is the cause of the breakup. Children are naturally egocentric—their world revolves around themselves. It is in a child's nature to order the world according to themselves. That is how they develop and form a healthy identity or sense of self.

The bottom line is the child's overriding fear of being left by you. We all have memories of losing sight of our mother in a large department store, or of our parents unintentionally forgetting to pick us up from school on time. Take a minute to remember the feelings you had when a relatively short episode of unexpected separation occurred between you and your parent. Now multiply these feelings ten or even one hundred times. That is very possibly what your child feels, initially, upon hearing about your divorce.

I say this not to make you feel guilty, but to provide you with a foundation of information that will help you understand and work with your child through this time of adjustment and change.

Helping Your Child Adjust to Divorce

It is helpful to think of divorce as a change. That may sound simple, but really that is what divorce is—a big change, but one that children can adjust to.

With divorce comes the obvious, monumental change of the parents splitting up and going their separate ways. Then there is the likelihood that your child will have to move to another residence and go back and forth between mom's house and dad's house. Your child may have to change schools, friends, and extracurricular activities. In some cases, your child will be visiting the other parent out of state. In some cases siblings will be separated. Minimizing these additional losses is always in your child's best interest.

Generally, except in cases involving domestic abuse or neglect, the more you can keep your child's lifestyle as close as possible to what it was before the divorce, the easier time your child will have adjusting to the divorce.

How Long Does It Take for a Child to Adjust to Divorce?

Many child psychologists and experts on divorce say that children take approximately two years to make their biggest adjustments to a divorce. The two-year period following a divorce is usually the time of the most emotional upheaval for children.

Of course, every child is different, and yours may take more or less time to adjust. Consider the developmental age and stage of your child, and his or her temperament. These two factors will make a difference in how your child adjusts to divorce.

Your Child's Temperament

Break up the word *temperament,* and you have *temper* as its root. The closest relative of the word *temperament* is *temperature.* So when I think of temperament, I think of a child's emotional temperature.

Do your child's emotions run hot? Is she prone to intense emotions? Does she have difficulty with transitions? Does she have irregular sleep and eating patterns when stressed?

Perhaps your child's emotions run cooler? Does she tend to adjust relatively easily to new people and new situations? Does she have low-key emotional responses for the most part? Is she easy to calm down when upset?

Maybe your child is in the middle of these two extremes. He or she may have emotional responses that are mostly on moderate. He or she may take some time to warm up to new situations and people but generally adapts pretty well. He or she may have varied, but not too chaotic, eating and sleeping patterns.

Psychologists have long called these three types of childhood temperaments: "difficult," "easy," and "slow to warm up." Unfortunately, these labels of childhood temperament can easily become associated with a child being either "good" or "bad." I mention them only because they are still in active use today to describe general characteristics of a child's behavior. No child meets the criteria for any one category all the time.

Although I know that most parents who have experienced the inevitable challenges of child rearing may have trouble believing this, the temperament folks say that most children (75 percent) fall into the "easy" category, meaning that they adjust well to new situations and bounce back quickly from hurts—they are resilient. Just 15 percent are "slow to warm up." These children are resistant to new situations and people and have difficulty with emotional regulation. Only 10 percent are considered "difficult," with extreme reactivity to new situations, difficulty adapting to routine, and consistently intense emotionality.

How Temperament Affects a Child's Response to Divorce

Temperament is considered to be an enduring part of your child's makeup, an inborn quality in your child. Temperament is not the same as personality, although temperamental traits contribute to the formation of a child's personality. While temperament can be modified or changed by environmental influences, your child's temperament remains more or less stable throughout his or her life.

Some adults tend to be more introverted or more extroverted. Some people prefer solitary pursuits over extensive social interaction. These qualities emerge over time and become more fixed as children grow into adults.

All children will have difficulty with divorce. As a general rule, though, children who are naturally more adaptable to new situations will have less trouble than those who have difficulty with new situations. If your child has a tendency to be withdrawn, he or she might do better in one-on-one counseling. An outgoing child might enjoy a group therapy environment.

Creating the Best Visitation Arrangement for Your Child's Age and Stage

Parents often ask me if their child will be more affected by their divorce at a certain age. Many people believe that a one-year-old is too young to know what's going on in the family, or that because their boisterous three-year-old acts so matter-of-fact about the parents' divorce, she is doing fine.

It is impossible to predict how your child at any given age will respond to divorce. It is inevitable that he or she will feel a sense of loss and grief, but there is no definitive data to suggest that a child of a certain age does better with divorce than an older or younger child.

Each child and each divorce are so different that behavioral outcomes are difficult to predict. However, you can make things easier on your child by keeping in mind key developmental milestones in combination with your child's temperament when drawing up visitation schedules.

Age/Stage	Milestone	Things to Do
Infants	Bonding and Trust	Consistency of care. If possible the infant resides with the primary parent. The other parent visits the infant in the primary home. Visits with the other parent are frequent, even daily, for one to three hours.

Toddlers	Separation and Autonomy	If possible the toddler resides with the primary parent. The toddler visits the other parent during the day for four to eight hours. The toddler has overnight visits if the child is comfortable, with the other parent in the nonresidential home (two to four per month) starting at age 3.
Pre-schoolers	Self-reliance	If possible the child resides with the primary parent. The child has an extended day visit with the other parent at least once a week. The child spends one or two weekend nights with other parent twice a month or more, if comfortable, in nonresidential home. The child accompanies other parent on short vacations, up to two or three days.
Early Elementary	Peer Involvement/ Sense of Self	If possible, the child resides with primary parent. The child has an extended day visit with the other parent at least once a week. The child spends two full weekends with the other parent per month or more, if comfortable, in nonresidential home. The child accompanies other parent on longer vacations, up to two weeks at a time, with phone contact with primary parent. If more vacation time is available, multiple one- or two-week vacations are preferable to one extended vacation.

These are only guidelines. You know your child best. When planning a visitation schedule, keep in mind your child's tolerance for separation from his or her primary attachment figure. Even when the child feels equally attached to both parents, it is still best to have a primary residential home for children ages zero to nine.

Children need a home base where they can put their roots down. Ping-ponging children back and forth between homes is not recommended as being in your child's best interest. Children who stay a few days at one parent's house and then another few days at the other parent's house have chaotic lives. It is difficult for them to maintain friendships and participate in extracurricular activities. Imagine how you would feel if you had to move every few days. Instead, try to create a stable, secure environment and schedule for your child so he or she can heal and thrive.

Promoting Healthy Adjustment to Divorce

Here are some ways you can help your child deal with the upheaval of divorce:

* Speak positively about the other parent in front of your child.

* Listen to your child.

* Understand your child's temperament.

* Understand your child's developmental age and stage.

* Establish routines and stick with them.

* Open lines of communication.

* Encourage expressive play.

* Remember that each child is unique.

* Remember that divorce is about change.

* Take care of yourself.

Other Losses

Loss is an individual experience that can range from divorce to the death of a parent, or grandparent, or even the loss of a beloved stuffed animal. When thinking of loss, it is useful to think of it as a separation. Children who are bonded with a person, animal, place, or object will feel the anxiety and desolation that are associated with separation from this person or object of attachment.

I remember my then-two-year-old daughter's full-blown tantrum when I put her "blankie" into the wash. At that age, my daughter could not tolerate the fear and overwhelming feelings of separation from her blankie for even an hour. After that incident I washed her blankie only when she was sleeping soundly and not entwined with it.

Blankies, stuffed animals, and other things your child attaches to are really extensions of you. I remember a boy of four bringing his mother's nightgown to preschool because he feared separating from her so much. And my mother has told me about the time a plane she was on stopped just short of takeoff because my older brother was screaming for his stuffed dog that she had unwittingly left in the airport lobby. The dog was recovered and all the passengers had a much more peaceful flight.

We may find these stories amusing, but to a child separations like these are monumental.

The Death of a Pet

Keeping in mind the temperament and emotional age and stage of your child, you may find the following suggestions helpful when your child is grieving the death of a pet:

* Gather snapshots of the deceased pet and display them on a picture board.

* Make a special place for the picture board, and set candles, flowers, or other meaningful items around it.

* If you are burying the pet at home, incorporate religious or spiritual ritual into the ceremony.

* If the pet is being euthanized at the veterinarian's office, ask your child if he or she would like to send along some of the pet's favorite toys or blankets or even food.

Once your child seems to be adjusting to the loss, you can start talking about getting a new pet, if appropriate.

It is painful to lose pets because they often become like members of the family. They are often already in the home when your child is born. Pets are associated with loyalty, protection, and unconditional love.

Getting a New Pet

Children will get through the loss of a pet and eventually be ready to think about adopting a new pet. My children, then six and eight, were ready for a new kitten about three months after their cat died. As is true for most kids, they had a loyalty conflict around getting a new kitten. They felt that in getting a new pet they were somehow hurting the feelings of our deceased cat. If your child is torn by loyalty to the first pet, try the following recommendations:

* Reassure your child that it is okay to get a new pet.

* Tune in to your child's signals telling you if and when your child is open to getting a new pet.

* Let your child know that his or her old pet will always have a place in her heart.

* Explain that a new pet does not replace the old pet.

* Help your child understand that the new pet will be different from the old pet.

The Death of a Grandparent

Some children are lucky enough to have an ongoing relationship with their grandparent or grandparents from birth. But in our mobile society, it is the exception rather than the rule that children have regular contact with their extended family. Fortunately, transportation and communication technology have allowed many children continued and regular contact with grandparents.

A child's relationship with his grandparents can be a precious, loving friendship. Grandparents are often thrilled to enjoy your children without the added responsibility of having them all the time. Young children are often drawn to older people and a close relationship develops quickly. When a beloved grandparent dies, the child's feelings of loss and grief can be tremendous.

How to Cope with the Death of a Grandparent

Follow the guidelines in the section above, "Promoting Healthy Adjustment to Divorce."

* Consider your child's temperament, age and stage of development, and personal and religious beliefs when including him or her in a funeral or memorial service.

* Consider your child's level of attachment to the grandparent. Know that the more attached your child was, the greater the loss.

* Make a commemorative shrine, or a special place dedicated to the grandparent where you can display photos, sympathy cards, and other meaningful items.

* Help your child write a good-bye card expressing specifically what he or she will miss about the grandparent.

* Make a list of the good times the child had with the grandparent.

What If the Grandparent-Child Relationship Wasn't a Positive One?

Grandparents can be less stressed than parents by the routines and responsibilities of family life and your child can enjoy their undiluted attention. Of course, this is not the case in every child-grandparent relationship. When the relationship is not ideal, grieving is often more complicated for the child.

When children did not have a good relationship with their grandparents, or when children were uncomfortable around the grandparent's illnesses, they may feel guilty over the death. They may wish that the grandparent would come to life again so that they could wipe the slate clean and have a new, more idealistic relationship.

Children may feel that they caused their grandparent's death because they were angry at the grandparent or wished them dead at times. When this is the case,

* Reassure your child that all of his or her feelings are okay.

* Encourage your child to find something good to say about the grandparent.

* Help your child to understand that the grandparent is no longer suffering from pain, if he or she was ill.

* Help your child to let go of feelings of guilt by using the play exercises in chapters 11 and 12.

The Death of a Parent

The death of a parent is the most acute type of loss a child can experience. If the parent was the primary attachment figure, the child will feel a deep sense of abandonment and anxiety. He or she will also feel anger, and all the feelings that accompany loss, to an enormous degree. Thankfully, this type of loss is not the most common type of childhood loss, but when it does occur its impact is tremendous.

What Helps a Child Grieve through the Loss of a Parent

* spending time with an attachment figure who has been close to the child since birth

* being close to other attachment figures such as teachers, relatives, and siblings

* cuddling and playing with pets

* expressive play

* consultation with a child bereavement specialist or counselor

* involvement in a religious, spiritual, or other type of community

* keeping material things that remind the child of the deceased parent—jewelry, clothing, etc.

* talking about the deceased parent

* remembering and celebrating birthdays and special days associated with the parent

I can't think of any other loss that can affect a child as profoundly as the death of a parent even if their relationship was not ideal. Any misgivings a child felt toward a parent who has died will be left as unfinished business for the child to deal with at some point in their life.

In the case of a parent's death, I would almost without exception recommend seeking the help of a professionally trained child therapist to assist your child in dealing with this loss. Even though your child may feel comfortable talking to you about the loss, he or she may try to protect you by not telling you everything, or you may not truly hear everything because you are probably grieving deeply, too.

Everyday Losses

Everyday losses are ones that seem minor compared to divorce or the death of a loved one. They include, but are not limited to, starting preschool or kindergarten, being excluded from a birthday party, being teased or bullied, and becoming hospitalized.

Everyday losses tend to occur more frequently throughout development than do major losses. In, fact each transition to a new stage of development creates some feelings of loss. At the root of everyday loss is the pain of separation—separation from a parent, in the case of starting school, or from a peer group, in the case of getting teased.

Everyday losses that remain unresolved—that is, the emotional charge that goes with them is never talked about or released through play—will accumulate and may cause your child to feel anxious or depressed.

Checking In

It is a good practice to check in with your child every day. I like to encourage family discussions around the dinner table, but this is not always possible with the busy schedules of extracurricular activities that many families maintain.

Bedtime is an alternative time to talk out the day (although complex feelings may come up during the discussion that may make it difficult for the child to fall asleep). Starting when my children were around ages three and five, they loved to get into bed and talk about their day, and then ask me to talk about my day. This became a fun ritual for us. Now that my children are of early-elementary age, I check in with them right after school and then again at dinnertime and bedtime. This is not an interrogation, but a gentle prompting to open the lines of communication. In fact, we make it into a game: I say, "I'll tell you one thing I did before lunch, then you can tell me something you did before lunch." Next, I say, "I'll tell you something that happened to me at lunchtime, then you can tell me something that happened to you at lunchtime." Breaking the day into sections can help your child remember the day's events and organize them in his or her mind.

Loss cannot be measured. Every child has his or her own way of responding to loss. What may seem like a relatively minor loss to one child can seem monumental to another. Dealing with more than one loss at a time increases a child's stress level. Having a stable, loving family and home environment helps children adjust to a loss more easily than they would in a chaotic and disorganized environment.

Remember to be gentle with yourself and with your child when confronted with loss and grief. Loss is a normal life experience. Healing and growth can come out of seemingly devastating experiences.

7

How to Speak Your Child's Language

Communication is more than words. In fact, most psychologists say that just 8 percent of communication is verbal. The remaining 92 percent of communication is nonverbal. Facial gestures, body language, and tone of voice communicate more than the content of the spoken word. The saying "the body speaks its mind" is important to remember when addressing your child. Your nonverbal signals tell the child much more than you may realize about your true feelings.

By age five, children are skilled at using social cues to predict, interpret, and influence the behavior of others. Guess how they learn these skills—from their parents! The request "Please pick up your room" can be interpreted in a myriad of ways by your child depending on whether it is said in an angry or friendly tone of voice. Are you yelling and pointing your finger in the direction of the bedroom or calmly issuing a request?

Table 2: Common Negative Communication Results

When Adults:	Children Feel:
Threaten	Intimidated
Command	Worthless
Preach	Inadequate
Lecture	Incompetent
Shame	Guilty
Yell	Frightened
Hit	Terrified
Make fun	Ashamed
Neglect	Sad
Invalidate	Unimportant

Seven Healthy Ways to Communicate with Your Child

The following are seven tried and true ways to communicate with children of all ages and stages. This style of communication builds a foundation of trust and respect between you and your child.

Listening

Listen to what your child is saying and how he or she is playing.

Listening sends a message of acceptance to your child. Get down on his level so you can make eye contact and read his physical cues. Observe his play. Is it angry? Restrained? Spontaneous?

Joyful? Destructive? Learn to listen to what is being said and what isn't being said.

Children will often avoid eye contact or begin fidgeting when they are afraid to tell you something. They may act out their feelings by destroying something they have made or conversely by nurturing a stuffed animal. Get to know your child's nonverbal cues. He is trying to tell you something.

Encouraging

Encourage your child to communicate by validating his or her experience.

Validation is letting your child know that what she is expressing to you in words or actions is real and meaningful to her and that you get it. Validation involves stating what you are observing in your child.

For example, to a child who is sulking because she didn't get invited to a classmate's birthday party, you might say, "I can see that you are feeling disappointed and left out." This is a nonjudgmental statement of the facts, which opens the door for your child to tell you more.

Ask Open-Ended Questions

Give your child a chance to express him- or herself.

One of the most common ways to shut down communication with your child is to ask questions that begin with "what" and "why": "Why did you draw on the wall?" or "What are you feeling right now?" Parents need to ask these kinds of questions at times, but children usually don't know why they are misbehaving, what they are having trouble communicating, or why they are pursuing a certain activity. It takes logical and abstract thinking to answer "why" questions; children are just beginning to develop logical thinking around age seven. Children may experience tension and anxiety in feeling that they need to please you by giving a concrete answer.

Asking a child "What is it?" in reference to a drawing, for example, can easily shut her down. Often children create simply to create and do not have a preconceived notion of what it is they are making.

A more effective way to elicit further response from your child is to say something like "Would you like to tell me about your drawing?" This is an open-ended question that allows for much greater latitude in responsiveness.

Door Openers

Invite your child to communicate.

Door openers are simple validating phrases that let your child know you are with them. They are nonintrusive comments; they don't interrupt your child's thought or play process but facilitate and encourage greater expression.

Examples of door openers are "I see that you are working very hard on your picture," "I notice that you are using the red crayon," and "Can you tell me about what the family is doing in the dollhouse?"

"I" Statements

Use "I" statements versus "You" statements.

Statements beginning with "you," such as "You made a mess," or "You look so sad," communicate blame and the assumption that you know what your child is feeling or doing.

Using statements beginning with "I feel," "I think," "I notice," or "I understand" communicates respect—"I understand that you had fun painting but now it's time to clean up," or "I think you might be feeling sad." Modeling "I" statements for your child is an invaluable communication skill that he will use for the rest of his life.

Speak to Your Child's Developmental Age

Use communication skills consistent with your child's developmental stage.

Using complex sentences with a two-year-old, for example, will guarantee that your message will go in one ear and out the other. Two-year-olds are just learning to put a few words together. Use age-appropriate language, e.g., "Mommy is going bye-bye for a little while," rather than "I have to go to the store now to pick up some milk and I'll be back soon." Similarly, avoid using baby talk with older children, because it is disrespectful and demeaning.

Use Playful and Respectful Communication Methods

Find creative ways to communicate with your child.

Puppets, toy phones, writing each other secret messages, and drawing pictures are all creative ways of communicating.

Words are not necessarily the best or most powerful tools for getting your point across. Remember that your child's language is play. Using play as a means to open up communication can work in the same way as when adults make a quilt together or share some common activity that opens up an active dialogue. Get out the clay and play with your child. It can be amazing what you find out about yourself and your child.

8

What Is Play Therapy?

There is no better way for children to express their feelings than through play. Through play children make sense of their world in a safe way, develop physical and mental skills, hone their imagination, and increase their repertoire of social skills.

Play is a child's language. Through play children can test reality—that is, they can experiment with problem solving and playing out real-life scenarios in a world of make-believe. A child may dress up like a firefighter, play the role of the mother in a dollhouse, or build an ideal world in a sandtray. With play, the possibilities are limitless.

What Is Play Therapy?

Play therapy is a hands-on approach to gaining insight into a child's world through his or her primary means of communication, play.

Play is a comfortable and familiar way for a child to organize and express the chaotic feelings of loss and grief. A child may be unaware of what she is feeling until it comes out in play therapy. A grieving child may start with a hunk of clay and begin to gently knead it. Within minutes she may be pounding the clay with a fist or a rubber mallet and expressing a great deal of anger.

Kim's Story: Playing Out the Death of Her Father

Kim was a six-year-old girl whose father died in a car accident. A few days before the accident, Kim and her father had argued over Kim's refusal to wear her coat outside. Because she was adamant about not wearing the coat, and because she had a cold and the weather was rainy, her father had insisted that his daughter stay indoors. Kim stomped into her room and said, under her breath, "I hate you, Daddy," wishing her dad would leave her alone.

A short time afterward, Kim heard the news that her father had died in the car accident.

Kim withdrew and would not come out of her room for hours at a time. She refused dinner and stopped talking completely.

Kim had always loved to paint, so her mother put out her paints in hopes that they might draw her daughter out of her silent suffering. Sure enough, Kim painted a self-portrait but blackened the entire picture with so much paint that the paper ripped and fell off the easel in shreds.

When Kim's mother asked her daughter if she would like to say anything about her picture, Kim said, "This is me being a bad girl."

What Is Kim Trying to Say through Her Play?

By painting a picture of herself and then blacking out her portrait, Kim was attempting to distance herself from her feelings. Clearly Kim was feeling guilty and responsible for her father's death. Her feelings were so strong that they seemed intolerable to her, and she felt that if she didn't exist symbolically (blacking herself out) then her feelings wouldn't exist either.

Further inquiry from Kim's mother led Kim to discover that she saw herself as bad and out of control, believing she had caused her father's death by saying, "I hate you," during their argument and wishing her father would "just disappear."

Kim's mother, once she was aware of her daughter's feelings, was able to reassure her that her father's death was not her fault and that it was okay to feel all of her feelings and then move through them. Kim, with the help of her mother, was able to express her sadness and guilt over the loss of her father and remember how much she meant to him.

Kim's mother was doing what a play therapist would do: finding a medium through which the child could express her complex inner feelings. Through the use of paint, Kim was able to organize her chaotic feelings into a clear statement. This is just one example of how you can help your child through play at home using some of the techniques that child therapists use.

Types of Play Therapy

There are two types of play therapy: nondirective and directive.

Nondirective Play Therapy

In nondirective play therapy the child therapist doesn't sit back and simply observe the play in a passive way. In fact, the therapist is actively attuned, listening and observing and making comments that will elicit greater expression of feeling, or pacing the play so that powerful emotions do not overwhelm the child all at once. Nondirective play that occurs in a professional setting allows the child to explore the play therapy environment and gravitate to an activity, toy, or game that interests him or her. The therapist's role is to listen, observe, note the symbolic actions of the play, and help the child learn to regulate his or her emotional state. The therapist remains supportive and present but nonintrusive, following the child's lead and not his or her own preconceived agenda.

It is not recommended that parents use nondirective play at home, because this type of therapy draws largely on bringing material from the subconscious into the conscious mind, and because it is child-directed and does not require the kind of structure that directive play therapy does. These two factors can make nondirective play therapy overwhelming to children and parents. Depressed and traumatized children are especially prone to explosive emotional release at some point during the play therapy process and need the expertise of trained professionals, such as child psychologists, counselors, and psychiatrists, to help interpret and contain their emotions. And, for parents who are already intensely emotionally involved with their children, it can be difficult to separate out their own feelings from those of their child. Trained professionals spend years studying the symbolic and thematic meaning of child's play in this context and are able to contain the inevitable emotional storms that arise.

Directive Play Therapy:

Directive play is what you will be learning to do with your child at home to help care for him or her during the grieving process. Directive play therapy involves the parent or therapist's taking an active role in the play and structuring the playtime for a specific purpose. If your child is angry, you might try "clay play" (page 53), which has detailed directives and expected, but not guaranteed, outcomes. If your child is feeling insecure you may guide him or her in the "circle of support" exercise (page 131). It is hoped that these directives will help alleviate the sadness or the anger, but of course it is impossible to predict the outcome, because each child has a unique personality and temperament that will influence the way a specific directive works for them.

In my experience, parents who use directive play therapy techniques at home consistently report a positive outcome of some kind—either alleviating stress and tension in their child, or helping their child to organize the tangle of emotions that come with loss.

Directive play puts the parent and child in charge and automatically contains the play by putting a boundary around it. There is a focus and purpose to each directive or play exercise. The principle behind directive play is much like the idea behind consistency in parenting. You are providing a structured and safe environment for your child to express his or her feelings and giving a specific tool with which to do so.

Sometimes parents worry that directive play will limit their child's spontaneity and freedom of expression. Actually, the opposite is true. Within the context of a structured, predictable exercise, the child feels free to express and regulate the depth of feeling that he or she is most comfortable with.

Play therapists may also use a more directive approach if non-directive methods prove too overwhelming for the child, or if a child is so depressed or traumatized that he or she has stopped playing altogether. Directive play can help to jump-start the healing process of play again.

Some children have never learned how to play or been allowed to play and need to be encouraged. Directive play can be used for this purpose. It can also be a diagnostic tool in certain instances. Directive play allows you to observe the type and quality of your child's play. Does your grieving child prefer to play alone or with others? Does he play in a chaotic or organized way, or does he not play at all? When observing your child, you can also take note of how his play has changed since the loss occurred. These observations can help you better understand your child's feelings.

The Play Therapy Room

Play therapy rooms used in counseling are set up to provide a sense of physical and emotional safety. They are usually rather small areas that create a womblike feeling. You have no doubt seen your child making a "fort" by covering a table with a sheet. Children need a private place where they can let go, just as adults need a quiet time and place each day to unwind. Toys, activities, and materials are carefully chosen by the play therapist to encourage expression of feelings and to facilitate the symbolic enactment of difficulties the child is experiencing.

The Language of Childhood Is Play

In the first few months of life, babies are entranced by gazing at their parents' loving faces. By eighteen months of age, dropping objects from the highchair and having you pick them up is a favorite game. By twenty-four months a child has discovered the joys of imaginative play and parallel play.

At preschool, two-year-old Dylan immerses himself in racing cars along the carpet. Next to him, his buddy Scott is engaged in the very same activity. These two boys are engaged in what is called "parallel play." Children at this age often play side by side without directly interacting with each other. It is a well-known fact that toddlers don't like to share. Parallel play is one way that toddlers protect their turf and learn mastery and control of their own world as they begin to separate from their parents.

Three-year-old Molly makes "soup" out of rocks and seaweed she collects on the beach. She uses a stick to stir her soup in a sand pail and serves it to her mom, saying "Hot." To adults this may seem like an unimportant activity, but, in this simple act, Molly's brain is stimulated, creating the connection between neurons necessary for more complex thinking later in life. She is mastering her external world and making it meaningful.

The Developmental Stages of Play

The stages of play described below occur on a flexible time line. The types of play often overlap; older children can be seen engaged in play more common to younger children and vice versa. These are simply guidelines regarding what you might expect to see your child doing at a certain age.

Parallel Play

Most commonly observed during the toddler years, ages 18 months–3 years

* Children play side by side, but not with one another.

* Children may imitate each other's play.

* Children are the narrators of their own play.

The Benefits of Parallel Play

* Increased self-reliance or autonomy

* Mastery over their external world

* Self-confidence as a result of mastery

Associative Play

(Most commonly observed in three- to four-year-olds)

* Children play together, but toward separate goals.

* Children engage in the same, but separate, activities like drawing a picture side by side.

* Children comment on each other's play.

Benefits of Associative Play

* Learning how to share

* Learning tolerance of differences (e.g., Jonny's drawing is different from mine)

* The beginnings of learning empathy through social interaction and awareness and acceptance of differences

* Increased sense of self or identity

Cooperative Play

(Observed in children over the age of four)

* Children play together toward a common goal.

* Children work together on the same activity (e.g., building a sand castle).

* Children communicate verbally in order to achieve a goal.

Benefits of Cooperative Play

* Development of problem-solving skills

* Development of pro-social behavior

* Development of complex language skills to convey ideas

Themes in Childhood Play

Symbolic play and pretend play are present from about the age of two and are such important and powerful elements of play that they remain present into adulthood, becoming more elaborate and sophisticated throughout developmental stages. No matter how sophisticated, our play retains the themes of early childhood play that include control, mastery, and making meaning out of our world.

When Molly makes her stone soup, she is using inedible objects to represent food. She is playing at make-believe. When Dylan races his cars, he is feeling powerful and in control of his world. He imagines that he is his daddy driving his car to work.

Seven-year-old Bobby dresses up in a black cape and mask and pretends to be Zorro. Five-year-old Laurie uses her toy doctor's kit to fix her broken doll and imagines herself as a doctor. In this way children experiment with adult roles and responsibilities.

As adults, our play becomes more organized and sophisticated. We play tennis or cards, or we "play" the stock market.

The Importance of Symbols and the Developmental Benefits of Play

Symbols are words or images that stand for ideas. They give meaning to our world. Children use symbols in play to express their inner world. A doll becomes a child's baby, a toy train symbolizes a real train, or a symbol of power. Children use symbols in their play to represent their experience of the real world.

Words are the most sophisticated symbols we have to express ourselves. Children become increasingly verbal, usually putting two-word phrases together by age two. At age five, children typically experience a surge in language development and gain command of a ten thousand word vocabulary. But still their use of verbal expression is limited in comparison to the highly evolved communication patterns of adults. That is why play is critical to a child's self-expression. Play is truly the language of the child and must be respected as such.

The following three concepts form the foundation of the importance of play in a child's development.

1. **Play helps a child to organize his world.** A child plays with plastic farm animals and learns what sounds they make. He learns how a cow is different from a horse.

2. **Play fosters a sense of self.** As children grow they begin to separate from reliance on their parents and develop a sense of themselves as separate and autonomous beings. As a child masters stacking blocks or attributing gender qualities to dolls, he learns to understand and gain mastery of his world, thereby gaining a sense of competence and a strong identity.

3. **Play allows a child to ascribe meaning to his world.** Through play the child attaches meaning to life experience. He may play out a real family conflict in the controlled world of the dollhouse. He may communicate a need for nurturing by "cooking" in a play kitchen. He may express anger over the death of a pet by smashing down a block tower.

Play: The Universal Language

Play is the universal language of childhood, which crosses all cultural and socioeconomic barriers. Children in every country and nation, of every race, of every socioeconomic group, play. That is one thing that all children do. Even an impoverished child in a Third World country will invent toys and games out of materials on hand: a rag doll, a stick for drawing in the sand, a game of hide-and-seek. Play is a basic human need of the child to create and express and learn to manage their world as they experience it through all of their senses.

Through play, children:

* develop their physical skills

* develop their cognitive or thinking skills

* learn to control their emotions

* express their thoughts and feelings

* make sense of their world

* practice social skills

* increase neuronal or brain development

* develop their imagination, which is a prelude to critical adult thinking

* develop and strengthen attachment behaviors essential to growth and development

In our age of high-tech wizardry, the rudiments of play still remain and do more to stimulate a child's brain and imagination than any computer game can ever do. And the expressive arts are invaluable tools for a child to use to learn to manage feelings.

The expressive arts, including drawing, painting, writing, music, and a host of others:

* are what make us most human and complete

* reach children who otherwise might not be reached, such as hearing- or visually impaired or cognitively challenged children

* connect children to each other in ways they universally understand

* promote unity and harmony

* tap into the subconscious need to express repressed or frightening feelings such as the fear of death or abandonment

9

Setting Up Your
At-Home Play Space

No doubt, if you're anything like me, a parent with young children, every room in your house or apartment is littered with toys, papers, and crayons, with Play-doh ground into the carpet. Maybe you're more organized than I am and your child's toys are neatly stacked in shelves and put in a toy box. As one mom said to me, keeping the children's play area clean is like trying to shovel snow in a blizzard.

What's So Important about Making a Special Play Space?

Q: We have toys all over the house. Why do I need a certain play area to help my child through their grieving process?

A: This is an excellent question, one I asked myself when creating a play space. The rationale behind making a special play space to work on issues of grieving is that your child can "put her feelings in a box." Making a play space that is separate from the rest of the child's usual play areas puts a boundary around what is done there. When you and the child leave, you "close the door," so to speak. A play space allows you and your child to engage in a specific play activity designed to help work through feelings associated with grief and then leave them there, much like putting objects in a box and closing the lid.

Just as many adults have quiet, sacred spaces for meditation, prayer, or renewal, this is your child's sacred space.

Q: Do I need a separate room for a play space?
A: Absolutely not. Any corner of an existing playroom, a portion of a family room or office, or even a toy kit in a box can be used.

Q: Do I have to buy a whole bunch of expensive new toys?
A: No. In fact, the in-home play program described in this book is designed to use materials that can be found or made at home or that cost less than $5.

Q: Can I use toys we already have in the house?
A: It is better, if possible, to use toys that your child hasn't played with before. I recommend using items that you can find at thrift stores or garage sales or ones that you can put together from household items. If you can afford to buy the materials on the toy list that follows, that's fine. But it is not necessary to spend a lot of time and money collecting items. The idea is to separate the grieving tools from the child's other toys so she doesn't associate grief with her everyday toys.

Q: But what if my child wants his favorite teddy bear?
A: That's totally fine. Let your child be the guide. It is helpful, and not harmful, for your child to gravitate toward a well-loved and familiar stuffed animal or toy to help him grieve.

Getting the Right Stuff

As you begin to see patterns in your child's grief play, you might notice some of the themes below, which are common in the play of many grieving children. You will want to have toys and materials that speak to these themes or enhance expression of the feelings that go with these themes. The play exercises in chapters 11 and 12 are divided into categories that address these themes.

* aggression

* abandonment

* dependency

* building up/tearing down

* fear

* death

* good and evil (good guys/bad guys)

* nurturing and caregiving

* control and power

* rescuing/saving/heroics

Toy List

The following is an inclusive list of toys that cover the most typical themes of childhood play. These are the same objects that you would find in a well-equipped play therapy room. It is not necessary to get all of these items, but I recommend collecting at least the "Essential Items," below.

Essential Items

* a family house (This is what is commonly called a dollhouse, but I prefer to call it a family house and find many more boys will play with it.)

* small dolls for the family house

* an indoor sandbox

* cuddly dolls

* crayons or markers, paints, clay, and paper

* old magazines and pictures for collages

* child-safe scissors

* glue

* plastic dishes

* puppets

* doctor's kit containing materials such as bandages, medical tape, stethoscope, and toy syringes

Recommended Items

* replicas of wild and domestic animals

* sunglasses

* small toy cars, stones, tunnels, bridges, plus miniature symbols of life and death such as tombstones, flowers, trees, fences, houses, churches, temples, schools, people, and other items for sand play

* plastic knives, rubber mallet, cookie cutters, and rolling pin for clay play

Optional Items:

* blank audiotapes

* beeswax (sold in small blocks in all colors at art-supply stores)

* sewing materials

* an unlined, bound 8½-by-11-inch notebook

* feeling flashcards (index cards with the names of feelings written on them, accompanied by a corresponding image— the word *sad* written below a sad face, for example)

The Toy Kit

If you choose to make a toy kit instead of a play space, get a large cardboard box and fill it with these things:

* art materials listed above

* two quart-size containers of sand

* small dolls, animals, trees, bridges, buildings, and other life and death symbols

* doctor's kit and/or medical supplies such as bandages, tape, stethoscope, and toy syringes

* plastic containers of different sizes

Store the above materials in the cardboard box. When you use the toy kit, remove the contents and use the box itself as the family house, inserting cardboard dividers, or fill it with the sand, depending on the directed activity.

How to Make a Family House

Use a shoe box for a small house, or a box such as one that holds copy paper for a larger house. Turn the box on its side. Flatten an additional box, and cut cardboard strips to make room dividers and/or floors. A very simple house is most effective.

How to Make an Indoor Sandbox

Find a large, shallow box; make sure it is sturdy enough to hold a few quarts of sand. Alternatively, purchase a rectangular plastic container with a lid, available at home-supply stores and stores like Kmart. Fill the box with enough sand to bury small objects in, but not so much that it is overflowing. Two inches or so is fine. You can also use rice or dried beans if you or your child is allergic to sand. (The plastic container can also be used for water play.)

Note: If you or someone you know is handy with wood, you can make both the family house and sandbox out of wood. The sandbox should be a shallow, rectangular box. Paint the bottom blue with a lead-free paint that does not chip or scratch easily. The blue color is meant to resemble water.

How to Make Dolls and Puppets

Cuddly dolls can be made by stuffing an old sock and sewing on buttons for eyes, mouth, nose, and ears and gluing on yarn for hair. If your child is under three, draw a face on instead, to protect him or her from the danger of choking on buttons.

Puppets can be made in a similar fashion by using unstuffed socks and making or drawing faces with different expressions.

Small dolls can be made by twisting pipe cleaners together to make a body. Heads can be made by tying a piece of scrap cloth around a few compressed cotton balls and tying it onto the body with string. Glue felt or cloth clothing on to the body.

Feeling flashcards can be made by taking three-by-five-inch cards or cutting paper into three-by-five-inch pieces and drawing a face on one side and the name of the corresponding feeling on the other. For example, draw a sad face on one side of the card and on the reverse write the word *sad*. If you are more adventurous draw the whole body, expressing the appropriate emotion, instead of just the face. Understanding body language is key in being able to recognize and identify feelings.

How to Improvise Other Supplies

Toy dishes can be easily improvised by using empty, clean yogurt, sour cream, dip, and other food containers. Do not use glass or cans with sharp edges.

Sandtray miniatures can be made from materials in most homes. Look around in your junk drawer, garage, and desk drawers and you may be amazed at what you find. You can use Lego people if you have them, make trees out of pipe cleaners, make a tombstone out of cardboard, or find pebbles and rocks around your house or at the park. Build up a collection by visiting garage sales. Note: Small objects pose a choking hazard for children three and under (or for a child of any age who likes to put things in his or her mouth).

Doctor's equipment a few gauze pads, tongue depressors, and/or empty syringes used for administering oral medications, can be obtained from your pediatrician. Make a stethoscope by attaching two long pipe cleaners to a cardboard disc, one on each half of the disk. You want to avoid any strangulation hazards with homemade toys.

Family house furniture can be made from small household objects. Empty matchboxes work well for beds, tables, and other furniture. Try plastic containers, wooden blocks, small boxes, and empty thread spools—get creative!

Modeling clay can be purchased for two or three dollars at art supply stores. I like to use a harder clay because it requires some effort to soften it, which can release many emotions in the process. If modeling clay is not in your family budget, try out the recipes for homemade modeling dough below as a substitute. I find that the second recipe is less gooey and works best, although it makes less dough.

Uncooked Modeling Dough

4 cups flour

1 cup salt

4 tablespoons cooking oil or shortening

1½ cups water, with a few drops of food coloring added gradually

Mix ingredients together until pliable. Store in plastic bag in refrigerator.

Cooked Modeling Dough

1 cup flour

½ cup salt

2 teaspoons cream of tartar

1 cup boiling water with food coloring drops and 2 tablespoons of cooking oil added

Combine the first three ingredients. Add the flour mixture to the boiling water mixture in the saucepan or frying pan.

Cook, stirring constantly, until mixture forms a ball. Let cool. Store in plastic bag in refrigerator.

Salt-Cornstarch Dough

This is a white dough with an elastic, smooth texture. It's fun to play with.

1 cup hot water

1 cup salt

½ cup cold water

1 cup cornstarch

Mix hot water and salt in a pan and bring to a boil. Stir cold water into cornstarch in a small bowl and add mixture to boiling water, cooking over low heat, stirring constantly until stiff. Let cool and knead until smooth and pliable.

Getting It All Together

Parents with grieving children are usually, on some level, grieving themselves. When you are grieving, the last thing you want to do is spend a lot of time and energy finding or putting together special toys and materials. It is a good idea to start putting some of these materials together before you are faced with a loss or a death so you have them on hand when you need them. Remember that loss doesn't necessarily mean the death of a family member or pet; it can be your child getting teased at school and feeling rejected. Loss comes in many shapes and forms.

You do not have to get everything on the toy list in order to facilitate healing. Use only the play materials and exercises that you feel comfortable with. There are no cardinal rules when it comes to healing from grief.

Know that the relationship you have with your child is the most healing thing there is. No toy or art project can take the place of your warmth and security. You know your child best, so choose the materials and exercises that you believe will best help you nurture and care for your child.

How to Create the Play Space

It makes no difference whether you choose to use a box of materials that you store away until needed or more elaborate equipment like a full-size sandtray and family house. The important thing is to let your child know that these are his special materials, to use with your help when emotions are running high or he is having difficulty expressing feelings of grief.

If you buy materials, choose a dollhouse/family house with a simple design. The simpler the item is, without a lot of fancy add-ons like ringing doorbells and electric lights, the more easily your child will be able to project his own deep feelings onto the toys he is playing with. When a child projects emotions onto his playthings, he uses his imagination and stirrings from his subconscious to create a play scenario, which gives a parent insight into the child's thoughts and feelings. Toys that are equipped with all kinds of extra doodads present a preconceived notion of what should happen in the play.

Jonathan's Story: The Family House

When Jonathan was presented with a family house that was fully furnished like a typical home, with dining room table and chairs, twin beds in the children's bedroom, and a double bed in the parents' bedroom, he froze.

Eight-year-old Jonathan was grieving the death of his mother and the tidy, what-a-family-home-is-supposed-to-look-like toy house confused and angered him because his home life had been turned upside down. In fact, Jonathan later revealed that he actually wanted to turn the house upside down.

But when Jonathan was presented with a completely empty family house, with furnishings available in a basket nearby, he immediately created a scene that clearly communicated his feelings of loss and grief. Jonathan slowly and methodically picked out small replicas of a mom, dad, and two boys. The only room he chose to furnish was the kitchen. He then placed the two boy dolls (himself and his younger brother) together with their father on the floor of the children's bedroom. He placed the mother doll on the roof of the house and explained that she was "waiting there for God to pick her up." He angrily said that his mother "doesn't live here anymore," but his way of keeping her connected to the house showed that he was not yet ready to let her go.

How Jonathan's Dad Set Up the Play Space

Jonathan's father chose a corner of the family room and put a plastic box sandtray on the floor with enough space around it so the two boys could walk all the way around it (an important point to remember when positioning a sandtray).

The father made a family house out of an old box that had held copy paper. He chose Lego people and used household items like empty matchboxes for beds and tables, scraps of fabric and felt for rugs, blankets, and pillows, and collected empty thread spools for tables and stools, and plastic animals for pets.

Jonathan's father also gathered up art materials like modeling clay, and markers, crayons, and old magazines to cut up for collages.

When Jonathan's grief had resolved and he was done with these materials, Jonathan and his dad put them away in the hall closet, where they could easily be accessed again but weren't a constant reminder of the mother's death.

Rosemary's Story: A Stay in the Hospital

Five-year-old Rosemary had to be hospitalized for three weeks. This event brought up tremendous fears of abandonment for Rosemary and frightening thoughts about death. Her mother put together a toybox play kit that could be brought to the hospital to help Rosemary relax and work through her fears.

How Rosemary's Mother Set Up the Play Space

In Rosemary's kit, there was a doll, a baby bottle, and cloth diapers; a play doctor's kit; some containers of Play-doh; paper, crayons, glue; and collage materials such as duplicated photos of Rosemary growing up, and old magazines that she could cut up to add to collages. Rosemary's mother also purchased a small, inexpensive portable dollhouse that came with people and furniture and folded up neatly for traveling.

Rosemary's parents stayed with her as much as possible, but for the times when they could not be there, they made a relaxation tape for their daughter to listen to on headphones. (The making of a relaxation tape and other interventions to help care for your grieving child will be covered in the next chapters.)

Using the play interventions in the section of chapter 12 entitled "Letting Go," Rosemary's mother and father were able to help Rosemary get comfortable during her hospital stay. As you can see, you can tailor your child's play kit or play space to fit a specific loss. As I mentioned earlier in this chapter, it is not necessary to buy or make every single item on the list. Starting with even just a few things can go a long way toward health and healing for your child.

10

Your Turn

A Parent's Guide to Their Own Feelings about Loss and Death

We all have experienced loss. As adults we may remember the feelings of devastation and rejection around not getting invited to a birthday party, or the time we came home to find our pet had been hit by a car. I remember the time the principal walked into my fourth-grade classroom, whispered something to the teacher, and then pulled me out into the hall to tell me that my grandmother had been rushed to the hospital and that my mom would be at the hospital. Some of us experienced the terrible trauma of child abuse or neglect, or the death or divorce of our parents.

All of us have a different story to tell. And telling the story can be the most healing thing we can do to help ourselves get a grip on our unresolved grief.

Debra's Story: Talking about Tragedy

Debra, a young woman, was nearly killed by her then boyfriend, in the presence of her four-year-old son. In order to recover from this terrible tragedy, Debra needed help as much as her son did. Debra needed to "put on her own oxygen mask first" so that she could then be in a position to help her son.

While both Debra and her son saw me for professional treatment, one of the things that helped Debra most was to tell and retell her story. Just as children will engage in what is called post-traumatic play after a terrible event, playing out the event over and over again until it is resolved in their minds, adults will talk about the event to whoever will listen. Another way they may retell the event is by keeping a structured journal (see the exercise later in this chapter).

Present Grief Triggers Old Losses

When our children are grieving, we are likely to remember times of loss and grief in our own life. If your five-year-old child is experiencing the breakup of your marriage, you may remember what was happening in your life at age five. The memories may be pleasant or painful. Perhaps your own parents divorced when you were a young child. It is not uncommon for a child's experience of loss and grief to mimic our own childhood experience or stir up feelings of other losses.

As parents who are deeply attached to our children, we may find it impossible not to feel the pain that they are experiencing. Because we are empathic human beings, our children's grief can become our own grief.

It's Not What the Loss Is but How It Affects Us

Loss and death affect children and adults in similar ways no matter what the loss is. Divorce and the death of a parent or close family member are arguably the most deeply felt losses since they directly threaten a child's sense of security and play on his or her biggest fear, abandonment. But all significant losses create the same feelings of grief in everyone to a greater or lesser extent. It is not as important to differentiate between the loss of a pet and the loss of a grandparent as it is to understand the feelings that go with a broken attachment.

How to Help Yourself

It is essential that you take care of yourself so that you can take care of your child. The following activities may help you do so.

Keeping a Journal: The Autobiography of the Soul

Think of the exercises below as a mini-workbook that will help you understand your own feelings around loss and death, your coping skills, and your level of comfort with talking to your child about death; it will also provide other useful tools to help you gain insight into yourself so you can best help your child.

Grieving takes a tremendous amount of energy. I recommend that you try to spend ten minutes a day writing or drawing in your journal. Try to establish a regular time every day for your journal work. You need extra rest in times of stress, so if you don't have the energy to write for a day or more, just pick it up again when you are ready.

Materials:

* an unlined notebook

* your favorite writing tool

* colored pencils, pastels, crayons, and markers (optional)

Exercise 1: Exploring Your Attitudes Toward Death

Answer "Yes" or "No" to the following statements:

1. I am comfortable discussing death with my child.

2. I can answer my child's questions about death.

3. I understand how my child thinks about death.

4. I believe in including my child in funeral or memorial services.

5. I have strong religious/spiritual beliefs about death.

6. I think other people, such as counselors, the teachers, or clergy, should explain death to my child.

7. My child does not need to know anything about death.

8. I am afraid that telling my child about death will hurt him or her and make him or her afraid.

Exercise 2: Digging Deep

Pick one or two statements from the previous exercise that particularly brought up feelings of tension or uncertainty in you. Write a few sentences about why you answered the way you did. If you like, you can do this with all eight statements. Feel free to draw or color on the pages at any time.

Exercise 3: Rating Your Comfort Level in Talking to Your Child about Death

In your journal or on the fear scale below, rate how you feel about discussing death with your child. Then write in your journal about what the fear feels like, where it comes from, and what you might do to change your comfort level if you wanted to.

No Fear

Some Fear

Moderate Fear

High Fear

Exercise 4: Exploring Old Losses

Complete the following sentences in your journal.

1. I was _____ years old when I had my first experience of loss or death.

2. My parents _____ .

3. I remember feeling _____ .

4. I wish someone had _____ .

5. What helped me most in this hard time was _____ .

6. I am/am not over this loss because _____ .

7. When I think of my child's grief over _____ , I feel _____ .

Exercise 5: My Coping Skills

Write and/or draw about how you cope with death and dying. Do you use personal/spiritual/religious ritual and belief? Do you exercise, write, listen to music? Write anything that comes into your head about how you deal with feelings of grief?

Exercise 6: Drawing a Picture of Death

You do not have to be Michelangelo to do this exercise. You can draw a picture of a specific death in a realistic fashion, or you can use shapes, lines, and colors to portray death in general. You can draw cartoon characters, symbols such as crosses and stars, or things found in nature. It's wide open.

Exercise 7: Creating a Time Line of Your Life

1. Start at the bottom of the page with the place and time of your birth, leaving a few inches of blank space underneath to write about this. Go on up the page, writing the following headings: three years old, five, seven, nine, and so on, skipping odd years until you come to your present age. Leave some space under each heading. This may take more than one sheet of paper, depending on how old you are. It did for me!

2. Now go back to your birth, and write a few lines about what you were told about this day. Were you planned or unexpected? What was the weather like that day? What was happening in the world? Were your parents rich or poor?

3. Each day, fill in descriptions of a few ages. Put down what you remember best about each age. Many of us tend to remember traumas and losses; others remember happy times. For example, I remember being hospitalized for a kidney infection at age three. I remember getting braces on my teeth at age nine and feeling excited that I would have beautiful, straight teeth. I wrote about both of these events.

Exercise 8: Reviewing Your Time Line

Look over your time line and write a page or two about common themes you notice, or about any other impressions that come to mind. You may choose to take one year in particular and use what you wrote on the time line as a springboard to expand on your thoughts and feelings around that age. Take at least one loss on your time line and write a page or two on your thoughts or feelings around this loss.

Exercise 9: A Walk into the Future

Write about what you think you will be doing next year, in five years, and in ten years. If you are comfortable, write about when and how you imagine your life will end.

Exercise 10: Writing about Death

Write about your fears, doubts, beliefs, and feelings about your own death. Do you really believe that you will die? What has influenced your views on death?

Exercise 11: Writing Your Own Eulogy

Write a few paragraphs about what you imagine people will say about you after you die. What were you known for? What were your qualities as a person? What will people remember you for? This is a good way to get a sense of yourself and all the good things about you.

Exercise 12: Dealing with Difficult Emotions

What emotions trouble you most? Take fear, for example, and describe it in detail, including how it manifests itself in all of the five senses. Some people believe there is the sixth sense of intuition—include that too.

Exercise 13: Wrapping It Up

Complete the following sentences:

This is what I've learned about myself and grieving from these exercises: _____ .

Right now I'm feeling _____ .

Right now, I need _____ .

I would like to work more with the following exercises: _____ .

_____

_____

The purpose of these exercises is to help you better understand your own feelings and responses around grief and loss. Remember, death is not the only reason we grieve. A broken marriage, the loss of a friendship, a move away from a familiar town, and a child's hospitalization all have feelings of grief associated with them. Please use this journal whenever you feel that you need someone to hear your innermost thoughts.

Getting a handle on your own grief will greatly enhance your ability to understand and help your child through his or her grieving process. It is so easy for our own emotions to be triggered by seeing our children suffering through the painful experience of a loss. It is not uncommon for parents to relive their ungrieved childhood losses when their child reaches particular ages. For example, a mother whose grandmother died when she was eight years old told me that she was flooded with memories of her grandmother's death when her daughter turned eight. Cataloging our life experiences of loss as adults, and gaining insight into the ways we dealt or didn't deal with those losses, will clear the way for us to better help our children with their losses.

Part 2

Healing Play Exercises

11

Specific Play Activities to Help Your Child Grieve

Play can be a powerful healing agent for a grieving child. Its power only increases when a loving, nonjudgmental parent facilitates the child's play. Playtime between parent and child has many benefits:

* increased bonding in a nonthreatening environment

* increased understanding and communication

* for the parent, increased knowledge of child development by observation

* increased insight into the child's feeling states

* increased comfort with a range of childhood emotional states

* recognition of the healing power of play

* positive and visible signs that the grief is resolving

Playing Guidelines for Parents:

Since you are the mirror for your child's feelings, try to remember the following when facilitating play with your child:

* Accept your child unconditionally. Respect and accept your child for being just as she is. She doesn't have to do anything to win your approval during this playtime. She doesn't have to perform or produce something to get your attention. You are there for her no matter what happens. When you accept her unconditionally, you communicate a strong message of emotional safety that is healing in and of itself. It is even okay to say, "I accept you for who you are. You don't have to do anything for me to love you."

* Listen with your heart. Go beyond the surface actions of your child's play and tune in to his feelings. What is he communicating with his play?

* Less is more. Avoid talking too much, since it can interrupt the flow of your child's play.

* Avoid asking questions or making suggestions, because they can sound like demands to your child.

* Do make brief factual comments, like "I notice that you are using lots of black paint today."

* Do not hurry the play. Let your child lead the way once the activity is under way.

* Wait until the end of the session to talk about the playtime. (See page 125.)

Play Boundaries for Children

When facilitating healing play with your child it is important to establish a few ground rules that will contain the play so that your child feels safe and knows what the limits are. Only a few basic rules are necessary. Too many rules will inhibit your child's play. Too few rules may cause your child to feel out of control. I have rarely seen a child cross the boundaries once they are clearly explained. My rules are:

* It is okay if toys get broken by accident. It is not okay to break toys on purpose.

* Hurting or endangering yourself or others in the play space is not okay.

Most children understand these rules and need only an occasional gentle reminder during the session, such as "Please keep the sand in the sandbox, since it could get in someone's eyes."

Consequences for Broken Rules

Usually a gentle reminder will do the trick to get your child refocused. However, if her anger escalates to the point of aggression, you can have her sit quietly away from the play space for a few minutes. I call this a "chill-out time" rather than a "time-out," which may have negative associations. After your child has had time to cool down, talk to her about her feelings—perhaps the play was too stimulating and she was unable to contain her emotions. Then switch to a more soothing play activity.

Avoid Getting in Over Your Head

If you are feeling anxious or overwhelmed by your child's emotions during a play session, chances are that he is sensing this too and is not feeling emotionally safe. At that point it's best to stop the play and do something else together, like read a book or go for a walk. If themes of extreme aggression or other intense emotions that make you uncomfortable come up, consult a child mental-health professional.

One parent I talked with became concerned when her daughter, Cindy, consistently put the mommy and daddy doll together in an embrace and made kissing sounds. The child's father had recently remarried and Cindy was getting used to a new stepmother. It turned out that the father and stepmother were affectionate in front of Cindy and she felt left out and angry. Cindy's mother had trouble dealing with her own and her daughter's feelings around this issue and brought her to a child therapist to resolve these issues.

When to Seek Professional Help

* Your child is stuck in his or her play. The same themes keep coming up time after time.

* The themes contain graphic violent and/or sexual content.

* Your child has been exposed to or experienced a traumatic event such as violence or physical, sexual, or emotional abuse.

* The issues that your child is dealing with are "too close to home." They remind you of something you yourself experienced and you are having trouble separating your feelings from your child's feelings.

Starting Out

When you have the play space set up and ready to go, invite your child to come into the play space. Ask her if she would like to play with you. Get her permission. Never force a play session—it is important that your child feel in control. If your child consents, and they almost always do, then let her naturally gravitate to what she would like to play with.

This is your child's special time. You are there as a facilitator or guide. Let your child choose an activity such as clay play or family-house play, and remember your role as a play partner—to accept your child unconditionally, listen with your heart, and not interfere with words or actions that disrupt the flow of the play.

As the parent, you are the safe container—you hold your child's emotions. Consider how you feel when you are listened to by a caring friend, spouse, or professional helper. No one likes advice or commands or interruptions while sharing from the heart. We just want to be heard and understood. When you listen to and stay present with your child during his or her playtime, you are acting as a safe, secure receptacle for your child's feelings.

Time to Play

Now that your child is eagerly awaiting a play session with you, what do you do?

1. Let your child choose an activity in the play space, or suggest a specific play exercise.

2. Be prepared for your child to change activities midstream.

3. Have fun!

Talking to Your Child After a Play Session

It can be useful to debrief at the end of a play session. Attaching words to actions is one way that children express themselves. The purpose of debriefing is to allow your child to communicate anything he or she might like to say about the play and to summarize or formally close the playtime. It's a good idea to ask open-ended questions. Don't be surprised, however, if your child doesn't say anything or says something seemingly unrelated, such as "I'm hungry." Below are some sample questions you might ask your child after a play session:

* Would you like to say anything about your playtime today?

* What was the best part of your playtime today? The worst part?

* How are you feeling now?

Play Exercises

I've divided the play exercises into four general themes that tend to show up in the play of grieving children. These themes may overlap. It is impossible to know beforehand how your child will respond to one activity or another. If you notice that your child is angry, it may be that he would do better with a relaxation exercise than with one of the "Feel Your Feelings" exercises. As with any relationship, it will take some time for you to negotiate the play relationship with your child.

During play, a wide range of feelings will be acted out by your child. You can expect to see:

* anger

* clinginess in response to fear of abandonment

* withdrawal—an unwillingness to cope with feelings

* panic—extreme fear of abandonment

* unfocused behavior—a feeling that the world has been turned upside down

* guilt

* hyperactivity or nervousness

* regression

* body aches and pains

Play can help by providing a safety net for chaotic feelings, a release for intense emotions, and a haven for letting go into relaxation and relief from everyday concerns.

Below are healing play exercises that you can share with your child. I've divided the exercises into four main categories:

1. Feel Your Feelings

2. Tell the Story

3. Work It Out

4. Let It Go

Remember that these categories can overlap. For example, clay play can be used for both "Feel Your Feelings" and "Work It Out."

Feel Your Feelings

Identifying our feelings is the first step in healing. For a child to name what he is feeling gives him a sense of mastery over the feeling. The exercises below are designed to help children get a sense of exactly what they are feeling in their grief process. The exercises are child-friendly and easy to use at home.

Play Exercise 1:
Body Tracing

Materials:

One large sheet of paper big enough for your child to lie down on (butcher paper works great, or staple or tape together several large grocery or shopping bags). Alternative: Use sidewalk chalk and do this outside in a safe place on a smooth concrete or paved surface.

Ready, Set, Go:

Ask your child to lie face up on the paper or paved surface. Trace the outline of your child's body with a marker or chalk. Now have your child get up. Children will usually marvel at how big they are on paper. Next, let your child color the parts of their body that feel sadness, fear, anger, guilt, happiness, or anxiety. You may suggest different colors for different feelings. Some children will scribble in the heart area, indicating a lot of pain there.

Suggestions for Parents:

Pay attention to how forcefully or gently your child colors a certain area. Is he omitting certain areas? Ask him if he can say the feeling word that goes with the place he colored. If he can't, that's okay. You may ask him if he would like to tell you about the picture. Avoid asking "What is this?" or "What is that?" since your child will most likely feel that he is supposed to come up with a correct answer.

Possible Outcomes:

* The child develops an enhanced self-image.

* The child gains an awareness of how grief resides in the body.

* The child catalogs his feelings—mastery of the location of feelings.

* You get an indication of how intensely your child is feeling.

Follow-up:

This exercise can be followed up with some of the exercises in other categories, such as "Scribble Pages," or "Working It Out to Music."

Play Exercise 2: Feeling Flash Cards

Materials:

Three-by-five-inch index cards, or construction paper cut into rectangular strips; crayons or markers

Ready, Set, Go:

On each card draw a stick figure or face representative of a basic feeling state: sad, mad, glad. Then write the name of the feeling below the face of figure. Expand your repertoire depending on the age of the child, including betrayal, guilt, shame, abandoned, lonely, and so on. Let your child participate in making the cards.

Suggestions for Parents:

* Allow your child to select a card from the deck. Invite her to tell you a story about this person. Write down what she tells you and then read it back to her. Ask her if she wants to add anything else to the story.

* Pick a card and make up a story about a child (not your own child) who might be experiencing this feeling. Explain that all feelings are okay.

* Show a card to your child, cover up the label, and let her guess what the feeling is. This is not a test, but a way of increasing the child's feeling-word vocabulary. If your child doesn't guess the exact word, say "That's close," or "Try one more time," or "That's interesting. Tell me about how _____ feels."

Possible Outcomes:

* Your child achieves increased mastery over the grief by storytelling using feeling words.

* Your child expands his or her feeling-word vocabulary.

* Your child finds greater ease in using feeling words.

* You recognize what your child is feeling.

Follow-up:

This is an excellent starter play exercise. Once feeling words are mastered and incorporated into her everyday vocabulary, your child will feel more in charge of her emotions. You can model feeling words, by using "I feel _____." statements in everyday life. "I feel tired after such a long day. How do you feel?" Or "I feel happy that Grandma called and is doing so well since Grandpa died."

Play Exercise 3:
Feeling Blocks

Materials:

Plain, unpainted wooden cubes or empty half-pint containers such as those that milk or cream come in; duct tape; markers; paints.

Ready, Set, Go:

If you are using wooden blocks, you can paint a picture of a feeling face—mad, sad, glad—to start with, on each side of the blocks. This exercise is designed for younger children, ages three to five. For older children, let them help paint faces representing more sophisticated emotions, such as guilty or joyful.

If you are using empty containers, push the top down to make a flat top, and tape the top closed with something sturdy like duct tape. Cover all the surfaces with a sturdy paper such as construction paper or cut-up brown grocery bags. Use a marking pen to draw feeling faces on the sides, or you may cut out expressive faces from magazines and paste them to the sides of your cube. Start with faces that represent mad, sad, and glad (for children ages three to five). For older children, get creative and let your child participate in making the cubes. Draw silly faces on the blank sides of the cube or add more sophisticated feelings that your child can easily master, maybe guilty or joyful.

The advantage of feeling cubes or blocks is that they are manipulatives—your young child who loves to touch things can hold, twist, turn, and even stack these blocks if you make several.

Allow your child to handle the blocks and see what he does. Does he focus on one particular image? Does he talk as he plays? What is he telling you through his play?

Suggestions for Parents:

This is a free-form activity to get your younger child familiar with the world of feelings. Avoid asking "What is it?" thereby turning the play into an examination. Let your child explore and see what he comes up with on his own. Prompting his thought process with gentle guidance can be helpful. For example, if your child's dog died and you have a picture of a dog on one of the block surfaces and other blocks decorated with sad, mad, and glad faces, you could ask your child to match how he feels with the picture of the dog. Keep it simple.

Possible Outcomes:

* Younger children will learn to identify their feelings.

* Your child will become more comfortable and familiar with feeling words and learn that all feelings are okay.

* You will gain insight into your child's inner emotional world.

Follow-up:

Like feeling cards, this is an excellent starter activity. Awareness and identification of our feelings is the first step toward healing. The earlier we learn to identify our feelings, the better equipped we are to learn who we are and where we are going in life. Knowing what we are feeling frees us up to make choices. For example, "Oh . . . I'm angry. Now I can choose to work that anger out in a healthy way such as by pounding out the clay or I can choose poorly and punch someone in the nose."

Many adults I have worked with in my practice didn't have the slightest idea of how they were feeling at any given moment. When we don't know what we are feeling, it is impossible for us to express the feeling. Getting in touch with your feelings sounds like a cliché, but it is actually one of the most important behaviors that you can model for your child. Teaching your children to identify and express their feelings in appropriate ways is one of the greatest gifts that you can give them.

Tell the Story

Children who are grieving need to tell their story. They need to tell you what happened. The telling in itself is healing. Some children may need to tell the story one time; some need to tell it one hundred times.

Children tell the story of their grief in a variety of ways. They may use puppets or dramatic play. They may use journals and drawings and paintings. They may tell you verbally or through their behavior.

Storytelling has the advantage of putting feelings around a traumatic event into an organized form with a beginning, middle, and end. Initially your child's story may only have a beginning, or it may start with the end and work backward. This is all part of the process. Let your child's story unfold in its many different forms. Eventually you will see greater organization and healing as the child thought process around the event becomes more integrated, or organized.

Once your child has mastered some basic feeling vocabulary from the "Feel Your Feelings" exercises, he or she will be able to use that foundation to help create and tell his or her story. The following play exercises are designed to help your child tell his or her story.

Play Exercise 4:
Circle of Support

Materials:

A piece of unlined paper, letter size or larger; crayons or markers

Ready, Set, Go:

Draw concentric circles (like a dartboard or target), starting with a small circle in the middle of the page and three or four rings around this center circle. The circles get bigger as you move away from the center circle.

Have your child draw a simple picture of her face in the innermost circle and label it "ME." Now help your child to identify the people who care about her. Label the rings with the names of the people who care. Encourage your child to put the people who she feels cares about her most closest to the center circle. For example, most children, will put "family" as the ring closest to the center.

Continue to label the circles with "friends, teachers, religious or spiritual supports, relatives, neighbors," even "pets." You can always keep adding circles or put more names on each ring.

Note: The general words *family, friends,* and so on are printed on the ring at the top, with room for the child to personalize it with particular individuals' names.

Suggestions for Parents:

* If your child writes the name of a stepparent or someone you may not consider supportive, try to let it go. This is your child's choice. If you strongly disagree with the value of a support person your child chooses, bring it up at a later time. Now, when your child is feeling vulnerable, is not the time for value judgments.

* Sometimes a grieving child has trouble concentrating and remembering. If she has left out someone you know to be an important person or pet, gently ask her if she might want to include that person or pet.

* You can also ask your child if there is someone who isn't in her support circle whom she would like to be in her circle—maybe a counselor, or a group like Boy Scouts or Campfire Girls.

Possible Outcome:

* The point of making a support circle is to remind your child during a time of loss just how many people love and care about them. Post the support circle in the child's room or on the refrigerator so she can see how many people are there for her, surrounding her, in a circle of love.

Follow-up:

Periodically, you can review the circle of support with your child. Ask her to tell you the things she especially likes about each person. And usually with time, more support people can be added!

Play Exercise 5:
Telephone

Materials:

Two play phones (if play phones are not available, use your imagination).

Ready, Set, Go:

Position yourself so that you and your child can't see each other but you can easily hear each other. Ask your child if he would like to call you up, or if he would like you to call him.

Let the conversation be child-centered. Do more listening than talking. Let your child come up with the topic of conversation. If this is difficult and your child can't think of anything to say, start out with a safe topic, like: "What did you do today?" or "What is the weather like outside?"

Sometimes your child will initiate a conversation about his feelings of loss. Take this opportunity to be accepting and understanding of his feelings. Encourage him to say more, by saying, "Can you tell me more about that?" or "That is really interesting to me. I'd love to hear more."

Suggestions for Parents:

* Practice your listening skills.

* Avoid making judgmental comments.

* Avoid asking too many questions.

* Use encouraging words, like "yes, mm hmm," and "Keep going, you're doing great."

Possible Outcome:

* The purpose of this play exercise is to reduce the child's inhibitions in telling the story. Play telephones can really

help get a conversation flowing. For example, I had one boy in my practice who had suffered a great loss and would not talk about it. When we put our backs to each other and put toy phones to our ears, his story suddenly came pouring out.

Follow-up:

Don't be discouraged if at first your child doesn't talk directly about the loss or grief he is are experiencing, but dances around it. Most children eventually find using phones is fun and empowering. They feel protected talking when the other person is out of their view. Give it a few tries and see how it works.

Play Exercise 6:
Puppet Play

Materials:

At least two puppets or finger puppets (You can also make simple puppets out of old socks—see page 104).

Ready, Set, Go:

This play exercise is similar to "Telephone," in that it facilitates communication by using an intermediary, in this case the puppet.

Let your child choose which puppet she wants to use. She may want to use both. Then, you can have a conversation with the puppet(s), or your child may direct a conversation between two puppets herself, or you can do a puppet show.

Suggestions for Parents:

*   Most children will take on the characteristics of the particular puppet they have chosen. For example, a lion will tend to bring out strong, even aggressive behavior. A lamb may bring out more gentle behavior. Puppets that

represent people may display qualities of a person your child knows.

* Puppet play is powerful because your child projects or puts her own feelings onto the persona of the puppet. This is a safe way for your child to manage sometimes scary and overwhelming feelings.

Follow-up:

It is important to bring some closure or ending to the puppet play. If at the end of a puppet play session your child is left feeling stirred up or seems overly identified with the puppet, gently bring the child back to reality by saying, "Our playtime is up for today. Let's take off our puppets together and go back to being Mom and _____ (your child's name)."

Possible Outcomes:

* role-playing—the ability to "step into someone else's shoes"

* safe experimentation with different feeling states through the vehicle of the puppet

* ability to "try on" different identities

* a way to explore different aspects of the self (e.g., a withdrawn child may feel safer to express her anger through the voice of a puppet)

Note: Some children find puppets frightening, perhaps because they seem too real to them or for other reasons. In any case, if your child is at all fearful of puppets, don't introduce them at all.

Play Exercise 7:
Journaling

Materials:

Letter-size paper (approximately fifty sheets), crayons, markers, paint, stickers, collage materials such as cut-out magazine pictures, feathers, pipe cleaners, tape, glue, glitter, and other art supplies. Alternative: Buy an unlined, bound notebook, available at most variety and art-supply stores.

Ready, Set, Go:

Journaling for young children is quite different from journaling for adults. Instead of being filled with writings, your child's journal will probably be a collection of expressive art that contains more artwork than words.

Explain to your child that this is his special feelings book. In it, he can write or draw or paint what he is feeling. (You can write what the child dictates to you if he cannot yet write himself). Emphasize that this book is to put down on paper what your child is feeling around the specific loss, whether it be the death of a pet or divorce.

Suggestions for Parents:

* Have as many art materials available as possible. Some children are inhibited about drawing and prefer collage.

* Allow for plenty of "scribble pages." If your child gets stuck, encourage him to scribble. Let them know that there is no such thing as a mistake in this project.

* It is okay for a child to rip pages out and throw them away if he wants to. If he gets frustrated and says, "I can't draw!" encourage him to talk about his feelings. Guide him toward collage or other art materials.

* It is okay to make suggestions, such as "Would you like to draw a picture of Sparky?" or "How about drawing a picture of yourself?" or "Why don't you try listing the things you remember about Sparky."

Possible Outcome:

* The purpose of the journal is to have a specific place for your child to put down any and all feelings he may be having around the loss. The journal is something he can build on day by day or week by week as feelings change.

Follow-up:

The journal can be followed by a larger and more organized project called the "Lifebook" (see below).

Play Exercise 5:
The Lifebook

Materials:

A bound, unlined book such as a scrapbook; art materials; collected photographs, school awards, certificates, athletic honors, invitations, birthday cards, baptismal certificates, adoption papers, and any other important documentation of your child's life. Alternative: three-hole-punch heavyweight paper such as watercolor paper or card stock and tie it together with string or yarn.

Ready, Set, Go:

This is an ongoing project that tells the story of your child's life. Start at the beginning, with pictures from around the time of your child's birth. Build the book chronologically including memorabilia and photos from over the years.

Suggestions for Parents:

* Encourage your child to write or draw what she remembers about each era in her life.

* Encourage your child to include the periods of grief and loss, even though this may be difficult for her. Include photos of deceased pets and family members. Write down pleasant or significant memories about them.

* Be prepared for intense feelings to come up as you and your child remember past experiences, both pleasant and painful.

* Take your time—these books can sometimes take years to compile.

* Keep a shoe box handy for setting aside new photos and other objects for the lifebook.

Possible Outcomes:

* The child feels an increased sense of emotional security.

* The child gains a greater sense of self or identity.

* You and your child build a feeling of closure around the grief and loss.

* You and your child create a record of your child's history and her importance in the world.

Follow-up:

The Lifebook is most often used with adopted and foster children as a tool to help them gain a sense of their history. I find the Lifebook useful for all children as they develop and find their place in the world. The Lifebook is also an invaluable tool for working through loss and grief. You can use entries from the child's journal and incorporate them into the Lifebook. For example, a page or writing about a deceased pet in the journal may be consolidated into a paragraph pasted in the Lifebook under a photo of the pet. Additional pages in the Lifebook can be used to expand on that theme as the child grows older and retrieves different memories.

Exercise 9:
Before, During, and After Cards

Materials:

Paper, art materials

Ready, Set, Go:

Direct your child to fold the paper into some form of a card that has a cover, inside, and back. Folding the paper in half will accomplish this. Older children may want to be a bit more creative and make a heart, circle, or other shape folded in half.

Ask your child to draw a picture, colors, or shapes, or have your child glue collage materials, on the front of the card, showing how he felt before the loss. Next, open the card, and direct your child to create a picture of how he feels now about the loss. Finally, on the back of the card have your child express in art form how he would like to be feeling about the loss in two days, two months, or two years, whichever time frame seems most appropriate for your child's developmental age.

Suggestions for Parents:

* Encourage your child to use words if he prefers not to do the card in art materials.

* Colors, textures, and collages are great expressive mediums.

* Some children like to use comic strip "balloons" so they can have their characters talk. See if your child would like to do this.

Objectives:

* Your child gains increased confidence that feelings can change.

* You get a sense of your child's level of hope for change.

* You learn more about what your child is feeling at the moment.

Follow-up:

Before, During, and After Cards can be made at intervals throughout the grief process. Children can look back and see how their feelings have changed over time. After a certain point you may see the "now" and "future" images looking similar. Your child is moving toward how he wants to feel, which is, for most children, happy and balanced again.

If after two weeks your child continues to create images that are dark, disjointed, and chaotic and there continues to be a marked difference between the "now" drawing and the "future" drawing, you may want to seek professional help.

Play Exercise 10:
The Sandtray

Materials:

A plastic rectangular container or a waterproof wooden box in whatever size is convenient for you, with a lid if possible; fine-ground sand (white ornamental sand available at gardening stores is sparkly and soothing to the touch) or rice; small sand tools such as shovels; miniature people, animals, buildings, trees, and so on. (If you or your child is bothered by sand dust, try misting it with water from a spray bottle.)

When choosing miniature items, look for ones that represent things in the natural world—small replicas of domestic and wild animals, stones, shells, human figures, houses, churches, other buildings (blocks come in handy for building these), bridges, arches, cars, trucks, birds, trees, shovels, crosses or religious symbols, and even a coffin if you and your child are comfortable with this idea. Halloween is a good time to find items dealing with death—coffin-shaped candy containers, skeletons, and tombstones are usually easy to find in party- and craft-supply stores.

Ready, Set, Go:

Once you have put sand (or rice) into the sandtray and organized the objects nearby into groups, e.g., human figures, animals, buildings, and so on, allow your child to choose what she would like to create in the sandtray. Anything is fair play. If your child isn't sure how to get started, you might simply ask her to "create a world."

When it looks like your child's sand play is winding down, ask her if she would like to tell you about her world. With sand play, it is often useful to take pictures of the sand creations after each playtime because, unlike art, journaling, and other types of storytelling, the sand world doesn't last.

Suggestions for Parents:

Notice not only *what* your child is choosing to include in her sand play, but *how* she is playing. Is the play chaotic and disorganized or is it precise and well-ordered? Does your child enjoy touching the sand or does she prefer to use a shovel?

Notice what types of themes come up in your child's play. Does she set the domestic animals against the wild animals? Does she build houses for people and animals and then destroy them? Does she tend to bury objects or only play with stones and shells?

Look for a progression in the sand play. Some children with lots of mixed-up grief feelings start out by dumping everything into the sandtray. As time goes on, the play of grieving children

Danny's Story: Using Sand Play after a Car Accident

Danny, age four, and his mother were driving to the grocery store when a car ran a stop sign and broadsided their minivan. Danny was pulled from the car by a bicyclist who happened to be passing by, but his mother remained trapped in the car for several hours before she could be pulled out by the emergency team.

Thankfully both mother and son had only cuts and bruises, but the emotional impact of the accident affected Danny for months.

When he came to see me Danny would almost always go directly to the sandtray, take all the cars down from the shelf, and simply dump the whole works into the sand. As the weeks went by, Danny progressed into an actual replay of the scene, selecting the two cars that most closely resembled those in the accident and having them collide. The mom and the boy would always get out safe, but I noticed a great deal of anxiety in Danny as he was trying to rescue the two figures.

After three months of playing this way, one day Danny came to my playroom and parked all the cars in neat rows in the sand. He then made a road and had the cars drive around to form a circle. I knew Danny had reached a level of peace around the accident. His play had become organized; the forming of a circle symbolized wholeness and closure.

usually becomes more organized and thematic. They choose and maneuver objects more carefully in order to gain a sense of control over their world.

As you can see, the sandtray opens up infinite worlds of imaginary play. I find it useful to write down the child's tone and theme of play and also to photograph the scenes when they are finished.

Possible Outcomes:

* Your children can tell her story symbolically. She doesn't have to use words.

* Your child gets to feel safe working in the small, contained environment of the sand tray.

* Your child can use her sense of touch in sand play.

Follow-up:

Sand play can be revisited many times. Children are usually thrilled to see their work captured by a camera. If you choose to take photographs of the finished scenes, these can be included in a journal. Captions below each picture in a journal will tell a story.

Play Exercise 11:
The Family House

Materials:

A dollhouse (prices start at about $20.00); doll furniture; furnishings such as lamps, rugs, blankets, and pillows; dolls representing all ages and races; pets. Alternative to dollhouse: Make a house out of a shoebox or your toy box (see instructions in chapter 9).

Ready, Set, Go:

Start with an empty family house. Place the materials in another container next to the house. Then allow your child to set up the house to his wishes. No direction is needed. Only engage in play with your child if they ask you to. The idea is for the child to get involved in family house play and act out scenes on his own. Sometimes he may invite you to play. Ask him what he would like you to do.

Suggestions for Parents:

* Let your child initiate and lead the play.

* Avoid setting up the house as you think it should look. You might be surprised if your child puts the bathroom furnishings in the kitchen area or sets the scene up outside the house or on the rooftop, but don't interfere.

* Don't be alarmed if he doesn't put people in the house.

* Notice themes in the play. Especially in children of divorce I tend to see a large number of adult figures arguing, or unhappy threesomes with the children sometimes literally in the middle.

* Make factual comments to encourage your child's play such as "I see that you've put all the beds in that one room."

* Refer to the dollhouse as the family house. There remains a gender bias about dollhouses, and renaming the structure opens up the possibilities for expressive play for both boys and girls. I find that the name change encourages more boys to try this type of play.

Possible Outcomes:

* The child has a symbolic, nonthreatening way to tell a story or express feelings.

* The child gains mastery of the larger environment by working with the small, contained environment.

* The child get to express his identity and role in the family setting.

* The child gets a chance to act out in play what is going on in his life, which is especially useful for children whose attachments have been disrupted by divorce, trauma, or other loss.

Follow-up:

Like the sandtray, the family house is a tool for your child to express what is going on in his inner and outer world. The family house may be visited often, with you noting recurring and new play themes. Family-house play offers an excellent opportunity for you to observe your child's level of anger, frustration, or comfort with what is going on in his life. It is also a great tool for observation of the quality of play. Does your child dump materials haphazardly into the sandtray? Does he place only a few items in well-thought-out positions? I have noticed that children who are overwhelmed with emotion tend to make very chaotic scenes in the sandtray. Conversely, children who are holding back a great deal of emotion are overly controlled and tend to be precise and rigid in their sand play. Feelings can change rapidly in grieving children, and what you see in your child's play may vary widely from day to day.

A Word about Family House Play:

As will all types of play exercises, if you have a hunch that something about your child's playing isn't quite right, consult with a professional. For example, if you see recurring unexplained aggression in your child's play, seek the help of a child mental-health specialist.

Similarly, if you notice inappropriate sexual behavior in your child's family-house play, such as posing figurines in sexual positions, or children and adult figures interacting in sexual ways, consult a professional. Remember that children communicate through their play. It is always a good idea to have questionable play, and play that you feel uncomfortable with, checked out by a professional whom you trust.

12

More Play Exercises

Work It Out

Play Exercise 1:
Claydough Play

Materials:

Homemade claydough (see chapter 6); cooking utensils like spoons, cookie cutters, rolling pins, rubber or wooden mallets, pizza cutters, and butter knives

Ready, Set, Go:

If you have the patience, it is a great idea to have your child participate in the creation of this stuff. I recommend the homemade, not purchased, variety, for the quantity you can make, the range of colors and even scents you can add, and the length of time it lasts. My sister-in-law sent my kids a five-pound batch in bright green for Christmas and we still have it in the refrigerator, four months later. (The homemade dough does need to stay refrigerated or it will quickly dry out.)

Let your child choose how much or how little claydough she wants to work with, and let her work on a table or other hard surface. Have the utensils handy for her to use if she chooses. Avoid directing your child's play. Let her take the lead. Simply observe, unless your child invites you to directly participate with her.

Suggestions for Parents:

Claydough play is a favorite activity of grieving children. There is something soothing about sticking one's hands into a mound of soft dough, similar to the satisfaction that many adults find when gardening and digging in soil.

Working with dough does not require the same type of planning and organization that some children use when playing with a family house. Claydough is a great activity to use in high- stress situations.

Notice whether your child takes out great big gobs of the claydough or if she is afraid to touch the stuff. Does she seem squeamish and afraid or does she plunge into the material, carving it up with spoons and pounding it with fists or mallets?

It is okay to gently encourage a timid child to engage in play or an overly aggressive child to slow down a bit, but unless your child is showing signs of great distress, let her be. Your child is always communicating with you through her actions. It is al lright to ask her what might be needed at the moment or to make factual statements like "I notice that you aren't touching the clay." Try to stay away from questions beginning with "why," "what," or "when," because they generally imply judgment, however unintended.

Since children work so much through their senses and young children especially love the sensation of getting their hands into things, claydough play is a wonderful way for children to work out their feelings of loss and grief without the pressure of having to find the right words.

Some children will narrate their play. I've heard children as young as three pounding away at the claydough saying things like, "I wish Susie (their deceased dog) were here." They get so lost in their play that they don't even know that I am listening. You may find that your child expresses her feelings in this way while working with the dough.

Crystal's Story: Her Mother's Hospitalization

When Crystal was seven years old, her mother was hospitalized in an inpatient drug treatment program. Although Crystal had a loving father who was able to take care of her, she was attached to her mother and missed her dearly.

When Crystal first came to see me, she was extremely angry. She used four-letter words to describe her feelings, pounding her fist into the pillows of my couch for emphasis.

When she was introduced to claydough play, Crystal gained a productive outlet for her anger that would not only serve to help her get rid of some of her anger but channel it into a more useful type of energy so she could move on with her life.

At first, Crystal stabbed the claydough and pounded her fist into the blob of soft, cool dough. Over time, Crystal's play progressed from anger to neutrality in which she appeared unsure of what to do with the stuff, to nurturing. During one of our last sessions, Crystal surprised me by serving me a claydough lunch of green pizza and blue cake.

Throughout our playtime together I was available as an observer and a guide. When her emotions were running high, I would make a comment such as: "I notice how hard you are whacking that clay—do you want to talk about it?" Usually I wouldn't get a response, but sometimes I would. The important thing was that Crystal was working through her loss and grief around her mother's absence and was able to feel more in control of her emotions as a result. In effect, Crystal was working through the basic grief and loss stages of protest, pain, and hope: protest in the form of anger; pain in the phase where she was a bit lost in deciding what to do; and hope in the form of creating nurturing "meals."

A tremendous amount of inner working out of loss and grief occurs in what may appear to be relatively benign play. Some themes that you may observe during this type of play include creation and destruction, expression of anger, and nurturing behavior such as making pies and cakes and other food items.

Children are often physically and emotionally exhausted if they have really gotten into their claydough play. The effort of working the claydough and creating even simple objects can be cathartic for their feelings of grief.

Possible Outcomes:

* The child feels no pressure to "make something."

* The child feels no pressure to use words to describe their feelings.

* Physical and emotional action can release pent-up feelings.

* The "hands-on" aspect of this work is healing in and of itself.

* A sense of emotional integration can occur in the child, bringing feelings of greater peace.

Play Exercise 2:
Modeling-Clay Play

Materials:

A pack of modeling clay (available in most toy, craft, and variety stores for less than $5); cooking utensils like spoons, cookie cutters, rolling pins, rubber or wooden mallets, pizza cutters, and butter knives; a small container of water. Alternative: Buy bulk clay at a ceramics or art store by the pound; there are commercial brands of harder clay, too, which will harden when air-dried.

Ready, Set, Go:

Put out the materials on a table or other hard surface and explain to your child that this type of clay often needs to be warmed up by working it with the hands or rolling it on the table. It takes a few minutes before this clay is pliable enough to work with. The container of water can be used for smoothing the clay or for pouring into clay cups or bowls that the child makes.

This exercise lends itself to a parental directive—a specific suggestion you may choose to give to your child to help give him a visual sense of his feeling self. Suggest to your child that he roll out a small, flat pancake of modeling clay in one color, and then three more separate, flat pancakes in different colors in progressively bigger sizes. The last "pancake" should be big enough to cover all the other layers. Next, direct your child to roll a separate lump of clay into a ball the size of a large marble.

Take the smallest pancake and direct your child to wrap the marble in it, then wrap that in the next size pancake, and continue until the whole sphere is wrapped up and you have a good-size clay ball.

Next, comes the fun part: Slice the clay ball in two. Most kids will say something like "Wow! A planet!" because indeed this clay ball cut in half does have distinct rings like those of Saturn.

Suggestions for Parents:

* Invite your child to talk about the planet and what it means to him. Do the colors say anything to him? Does this remind him of anything?

* If your child has already done the "Circle of Support" exercise (see page 131), he may relate these layers to the circle of support, with the marble in the center representing the child, and the layers representing the people who love and support him.

* Another way to talk about the clay planet with your child is to discuss the inside self, with the various colored layers representing feelings that stick to us, like sorrow, shame, anger, or whatever your child is feeling. Your child can peel off layers that he doesn't want and replace them with other feeling layers. Or he can simply note the

layers he is "wearing" right now and think about the idea that the layers are protecting his inside self.

Possible Outcomes:

* Hands-on activity connects the child to a sensory mode that is familiar to him.

* The clay planet provides a visual representation of what your child is experiencing internally.

* The child makes some order of his chaotic feelings.

* Pent-up feelings are released in a safe and constructive way.

Follow-up:

If your child enjoys clay play, you can expand this activity by making it more structured. Suggest that your child make a clay face that resembles his own face, or that he make a clay family or an abstract sculpture that expresses how he is feeling. Ask for his ideas, too. Just keep it simple.

Play Exercise 3: Punching Pillows

Most experts in anger management now believe that punching a pillow is not always the best way to manage this difficult feeling. Punching a pillow does not truly get rid of angry feelings. It only treats the symptoms of anger, not the cause. Even so, I am including this exercise for use as a temporary measure when all else fails. Try some brisk exercise like a walk around the block first.

You can use the punching pillow exercise:

* when other play exercises aren't helping your child to manage anger, or

* when your child is in danger of hitting herself or others in anger.

Materials:

Soft pillows. Alternative: a punching bag and a pair of boxing gloves (prices vary)

Ready, Set, Go:

This play exercise requires close supervision so that the child's anger doesn't escalate or become destructive.

Tell your child that you are going to set a timer or use a watch or clock to time the exercise. Tell your child that she is to hit the pillow as hard as she can with her fist (or with her feet) for three minutes. Most children run out of energy before three minutes are up.

Suggestions for Parents:

* If the child stops before the time is up and asks how much time she has used, be honest and tell her. Ask your child if she would like to use up the remaining time.

* Make sure to include a cool-down period. Take some time to allow your child's breathing to return to normal.

* Be mindful of what incident may have triggered your child's anger.

* Try to have your child attach some feeling words to the experience.

Possible Outcomes:

* Anger or frustration is temporarily released.

* The intense emotion of anger is cleared away, uncovering other feelings that may be buried, like sadness.

Follow-up:

It is not unusual for a child to burst into tears after punching pillows. It is also not unusual for a child's anger to escalate after this exercise; it doesn't reach the inner emotional turmoil that accompanies grief, which cannot be alleviated with this type of quick fix. Excellent follow-up exercises can be found in the next section, "Letting Go."

Letting Go

The play exercises you will find in this section are designed to help your child find ways to soothe him- or herself—the child's equivalent of "taking care of ourselves." These play exercises are good to practice before an incident of loss occurs so that your child will be familiar with ways to find comfort him- or herself.

You are your child's greatest source of comfort, love, and security, and these exercises can help you help your child during difficult times.

Play Exercise 4:
Making a Comfort Companion

Materials:

Soft fabric such as flannel, cotton, or fleece; basic sewing materials: needles, thread, scissors; stuffing (cotton batting, lambswool, or fabric scraps). Alternative: Take your child on a special outing to buy a stuffed doll, pet, or blanket that is cuddly and comforting to them. It is even possible to find such items at a "99-cent store."

Ready, Set, Go:

Involve your child in picking out the type of fabric he would like to use to make the blanket, doll, or stuffed animal.

If you are handy with a needle and thread, that's great. I'm not so great at sewing, so I made my children simple blankets using flannel and a printed fabric, both of which they picked out. I sewed the two pieces of fabric together on a borrowed machine, and *Voila!* a blanket.

For instructions on how to make dolls and stuffed pets, consult your local library or crafts store.

Suggestions for Parents:

Chances are, your child already has a well-loved and probably tattered blanket or stuffed animal that he's had since babyhood. My son, now eight years old, still has his receiving blanket and seeks out what is left of it in times when life seems a little too overwhelming. If he already has a comfort companion like this, make sure it's available to your child.

Possible Outcomes:

* increased sense of security through "bonding" with a special comfort companion

* a sense of ownership through helping to make the comfort companion

* a decrease in anxiety as a result of cuddling with the comfort companion

Follow-up

Children can become quite attached to their comfort companion. They may want to make clothes, a bed, or a house, if they have chosen to make a doll. These accessories can easily be made from scraps of fabric fashioned into clothing, and a shoe box can be made into a bed, for example.

Lauren's Story: A Comfort Companion for Her Hospital Stay

Lauren, age five, was admitted to the hospital for a tonsillectomy. Although her parents had mentally prepared her for the surgery, Lauren was understandably still anxious.

Before the surgery, Lauren and her mother made a doll out of soft yellow flannel. It was a simple doll and did not take much time to make, but it was the very first thing Lauren asked for when she came to from her surgery—after her mother and father, of course!

Play Exercise 5:
Make the Duckie Move

Materials:

A rubber duckie. Alternative: a medium-weight book, or a stuffed animal with some weight to it, such as a "Beanie Baby"

Ready, Set, Go:

Direct your child to lie down in a comfortable spot on her back. A couch, a bed, or the floor will work fine. If the child feels cold, cover her with a blanket. (Even if she isn't cold, covering her with a light blanket will increase her sense of protectedness, which will allow for greater relaxation.)

Place the rubber duckie on your child's belly right around her belly button. Ask your child to breathe normally, and see if the duckie moves up and down with your child's breaths.

Then ask your child to take a deep breath all the way down to where the duckie is and see if she can make it move.

Move the duckie up to just below the rib cage, where the diaphragm is, and repeat the instructions.

Move the duckie up to the chest area and repeat the instructions.

Make sure to tell your child to release her breath after each inhalation. There is no need for her to hold her breath.

Suggestions for Parents:

* Make sure your child is comfortable.

* As with every exercise, ask her if she wants to do this one.

* Notice whether your child is taking shallow breaths from the upper chest or deeper breaths from the lower and midsection of her body.

* Share your observations of her breathing with your child.

* Try to guide your child to take lower/slower breaths from deep inside her body and then let those breaths out with

a whooshing sound. This encourages the deep abdominal breathing that is associated with relaxation training.

Possible Outcomes:

* The exercise increases the child's breathing awareness and a sense of how it relates to body relaxation.

* The child gains awareness of how anxiety creates rapid, shallow, upper chest breathing.

* Using the duckie provides a visual cue for children to gauge their breathing patterns.

* The exercise can be used as a warm-up activity for creative visualization.

Follow-up:

This exercise can also be used in conjunction with the body-tracing exercise (see page 127). You can have your child breathe into the areas of pain or tightness that she has identified in her body drawing.

When your child is feeling anxious and out of sorts, which is common during the grieving process, you can gently remind her to use lower/slower breathing.

Play Exercise 6:
Creative Visualization

Materials:

Your voice and your child's imagination

Ready, Set, Go:

Have your child do abdominal breathing as outlined in "Make the Duckie Move." When he seems relaxed, ask him to imagine a place where he likes to be that feels totally safe to him. Ask him what the place is, what is smells like, feels like, looks like. What are the sounds he can hear in this place? Is it warm or cool?

What are the colors he sees? Ask sensory-related questions to help your child define his special place.

Write down the essentials of the special place and then put together a story that uses simple, repetitive words, to bring your child to that place in his mind.

Read the story of the special place to your child so that he attaches to the idea of a safe place as an emotional refuge to go to when times get tough. You can also record the story on a cassette for use during times when you need to be away from your child.

Suggestions for Parents:

Use a soft, soothing voice when reading the special-place story. A parent's voice is one of the most comforting tools available to a child. Even early on while still in the womb, your child recognized your voice and the voices of familiar people who were and are important to your family. Your child came to recognize these voices and associate them with comfort and security.

A Sample Story Script:

Let your whole body relax. Breathe way down into your toes. Breathe into your legs. They are as heavy as logs. Now take a deep breath in and let it whoosh into your belly, filling it up like a gigantic blue balloon. Your body is getting really warm and heavy. Take a deep breath and let it go into your heart. Let that warm air reach all the way into your loving heart. Breathe in through your nose and out through your mouth. Hear the sound of breath like a soft summer wind.

Now go to your special place. I'll wait for you to get there. Okay. I see you there and I am right there with you.

You are lying on the warm sand. Your whole body is so heavy and relaxed that it just sinks a little into the sand. Your toes are all warm and toasty and the golden light of the sun warms up your whole body.

Smell the salt in the sea air. Hear the birds play. Smell the warm salty air. Hear the birds call to each other like friends.

Feel the sand as it warms your toes and fingers. Feel the warm, white sand. Hear the sound of the water as it rolls onto the beach and then rolls away. Water rolling back and forth, back and forth.

This is your special place. You are in your favorite spot on the beach by the big driftwood log. The birds call and the breeze blows. The birds call and the breeze blows and the sun is golden, warm light on you. The sun is golden, warm light in you. A warm, golden light all through you.

You are warm and cozy in your spot. You are lying on your special blanket. You are safe on your blanket. You are happy and safe and warm here in your special place on your special blanket.

Your breath comes in and out like a gentle, whispering wind. The golden light of the sun shines on you and all through you. You feel so happy and safe here. You can come here whenever you want. I am with you.

The sky is so blue and the air smells so good. The sand is so warm and you are cozy and safe, cozy and safe.

Remember that you can always come back to your special place. It is now time to wiggle your toes and fingers and wake up your body. When you are ready open your eyes. [Pause.] Your eyes are now open and you are here in your [house, room, school, etc.]. The air is fresh and cool. Your body is relaxed. You are strong and relaxed. You can do whatever you need to do. You are safe and loved.

Possible Outcomes:

* You are creating a safe emotional retreat for your child.

* The exercise facilitates deep relaxation.

* The exercise uses the imaginative and creative parts of your child's brain.

Follow-up:

The sample script above is meant for a five- to seven-year-old child. You can use a few different visualization scenarios for your child at different times. It is likely that your child has more than one safe and favorite place. It is best to use no more than two or three scenarios, since creative visualization works best with repetitive themes. With children under the age of five, I recommend sticking to one simple visualization.

Play Exercise 7:
Modeling Beeswax

Materials:

Small blocks or sheets of beeswax (found in arts and crafts stores and some toy stores); a bowl of cold water

Ready, Set, Go:

Instruct your child to take a piece of wax and roll it around in her palms. Quickly the wax warms to the touch and also releases a lovely smell.

You may direct your child to simply warm the wax with her hands and, if she likes, place the warmed form into the cold water to cool, or ask her to make whatever shape comes to her mind. The formed objects will harden up in the water but can be used again when rewarmed.

Suggestions for Parents:

This is an activity designed to facilitate soothing and letting go. Beeswax has a natural quality that is quite soothing to the senses. Beeswax is different from clay in that it is translucent and is often unfamiliar to children. Beeswax has a smooth and pliable texture that makes it easy and fun to work with.

An advantage of using beeswax with grieving children is that it is wonderful for making candles. If you purchase sheets of beeswax and some wicking, it is simple to warm the sheets lightly with a blow dryer or over an electric burner and then place a wick at one edge of each sheet and roll the wax into a candle. This candle can be lit as a commemorative candle.

Possible Outcomes:

* Working with beeswax is a soothing activity that calms the senses.

* The child receives a concrete demonstration of how things change—solid wax to malleable wax, then back to solid.

* The child has an opportunity to make a candle to commemorate a deceased person or pet.

Follow-up:

Displaying a candle your child has made can really boost her sense of self and self-esteem. Also, children who make candles can gain a great deal of satisfaction from sending the candles to the bereaved spouse of their grandparents or to another family that is experiencing a similar grief.

Other Play Ideas

Play is a child's work. Play is also your child's best and most comfortable way of expressing his or her inner feelings. There are limitless play activities that you can do at home to ease your child's grief. Often children are so shut down by a loss that it is difficult for them to engage in much of anything at first. The exercises in chapters 11 and 12 can help jump-start a child's re-entry into life, but, as with all things, timing is critical. It is best not to force your child to participate in an activity that he or she is not interested in. This will only create feelings of anger and resistance. Wait for an opening or a cue that tells you he or she is ready to engage.

For children who are feeling ashamed or guilty, I keep pairs of sunglasses around. It is amazing how a child will open up behind the protective shield of a pair of sunglasses. Young children especially think that because they have the glasses on you can't see them.

Similarly, I have had children tell me that they don't want me to look at them. They feel so much shame around a particular loss, or feel so much responsibility and guilt, that even the kindest look is interpreted as a judgment.

For these children, I offer to turn their chair around so that their back is facing me, or I tell them that I will respect their wish for me not to look at them while they play. Most children will eventually ask me to look at what they are making.

In this vein, it is often useful to create a private space somewhere in your home where your child can go and be alone. Covering a card table with a blanket works well. So do small indoor tents or playhouses.

When I talk to parents about their children whom I see in my therapy practice, I focus on the positives. No matter how difficult a loss may be and how hard and sometimes prolonged the grieving process can be, there are things we can do to help our children. Nothing can be substituted for the unique and loving relationship that you have with your child. As a parent myself I know that love and consistency of care are the most important things that I can give my children. As a professional I offer to you these play exercises as adjuncts to the healing process. I hope that they may be of help to you as you take your journey of healing with your child.

Endings

As I finish writing this book, I notice that my throat feels a little tight and my heart a bit heavy. Something that I have worked on for so long, something so personally important to me, is ending. The book is finished and I believe I am grieving.

When we engage in an activity or a relationship so intensely that it becomes a part of us, it takes on monumental meaning for us. As infants we begin to make meaning out of our world through our relationship with our parents. As we grow into adulthood, our identity is shaped by all of our past and current experiences and relationships.

As we grow and change we leave behind the old and acquire the new. In this ever-evolving process of gain and loss, there is an aspect of grief.

Grief is familiar to me. I remember my stepson, Patrick, five years old, when his father and I were first dating, letting me know in no uncertain terms that he came first in his father's eyes. On our first outing with Patrick in tow, he said to me, "I wish you would fall out of the car." My husband and I still laugh at this—now. At the time, I didn't think it was very funny, but I understood the adjustment my stepson was making to integrate me into his shaky world after his parents' divorce.

The children I have written about in this book are representative of children of all ages experiencing the challenges and delights of growing up. Every child is unique; each child has his or her own story to tell if we take the time to listen. I feel blessed to have known so many children in both my personal and professional life.

In *Caring for Your Grieving Child*, I have written from the perspective of a mother as well as that of a child therapist. I remember the sleepless nights with my daughter, who was a temperamental baby and wouldn't let anyone but my husband or me hold her. She refused the baby swing and the stroller and had to be walked in circles around our rental house from ten o'clock until midnight every night before she would fall asleep—for maybe two hours if we were lucky.

I remember my son falling and hitting his head on the corner of an easel at preschool and requiring the first of many trips to the emergency room for stitches. He was always falling off something or banging into something.

I recall seeing my daughter off to kindergarten and crying. I didn't feel prepared for this transition. It seemed a cruel trick to have to watch your child go from diapers to the doors of the orange school bus in what felt like the blink of an eye. Fortunately, my daughter did fine.

As parents, we are often unknowingly grieving the stages our children seem to race through and leave behind. All of the sudden they are almost full-grown, lovely beings. Where did the days of diapers and bottles go? Similarly, our children experience both loss and excitement as they grow.

In this book I wanted to look at both everyday loss and acute loss. The big losses can seem insurmountable—the death of a parent or loved one, a divorce. These are losses we prefer not to think about, the losses we don't want any child to have to experience. It has not been my intention to "fix" these losses; I don't have that kind of magic wand. Instead, I have attempted to provide a place where you can go, when loss occurs, to find comfort and hope and perhaps some tools to help you and your child along the path of grieving.

I have developed a relationship with the readers of this book. As I wrote, I thought of you often, struggling with the day-to-day challenges and joys of parenting. I have thought of you as the most important people in the world—parents; I have thought of you with great respect and admiration. Sadly, now it is time to say good-bye.

I will hold you and your children in my heart. It has been my pleasure to take this journey with you. As we conclude our journey, I feel the bittersweetness of something so dear to me ending, but also the satisfaction of new beginnings and what blossoms forth from me from having traveled this far.

References

Bowlby, J. 1969. *Attachment and Loss,* Volume 1. New York: Basic Books.

Children's Defense Fund. 2000. *The State of America's Children Yearbook.* Washington, D.C.: CDF.

Fassler, D. G., and L. S. Dumas. 1997. *Help Me, I'm Sad.* New York: Penguin.

Kübler-Ross, Elisabeth. 1969. *On Death and Dying.* New York: McMillan.

Martha Wakenshaw, MA, LMHC, is a child therapist in private practice in Seattle, Washington, specializing in play and expressive arts therapy. She is a board-certified mental health counselor with fifteen years' experience as a child therapist. Her previous book, *This Child of Mine,* was shortlisted for the Robert F. Kennedy annual book award, the world's most prestigious recognition of social writing.

She has written for lay people and professionals on how to identify and treat childhood trauma, as well as several articles on child care and community needs for a variety of professional publications. She served as center director in a therapeutic clinic of abused and neglected preschool children and as a family advocate for Head Start and the Shoreline School District. She is a member of the American Professional Society on the Abuse of Children (APSAC), the American Counseling Association, and Zero-to-Three, an organization that does early childhood development research.

Ms. Wakenshaw is also an award-winning poet.

Herman M. Frankel, MD, is director of The Divorcework Center at Portland Health Institute Inc. (divorcework.com), and an Adjunct Professor at Pacific University School of Professional Psychology. Among Dr. Frankel's publications are *Dealing With Loss: A Guidebook for Helping Your Children During and After Divorce* and *Los niños y las familias en divorcio ó separación: Después de la pérdida, la vida sigue.* He is the holder of the nation's highest honor for community health promotion and disease prevention, the U.S. Secretary of Health and Human Services Award of Excellence. In his current workshops for professionals, general audiences, and workplace groups, and in his current meetings and correspondence with members and friends of separated and divorced families, Dr. Frankel is particularly interested in learning more about the influence of friends and relatives on separated and divorced families.